Feminist New Materialisms

Feminist New Materialisms

Activating Ethico-Politics Through Genealogies in Social Sciences

Special Issue Editors

Beatriz Revelles Benavente
Monika Rogowska-Stangret
Waltraud Ernst

MDPI • Basel • Beijing • Wuhan • Barcelona • Belgrade

Special Issue Editors

Beatriz Revelles Benavente
University of Granada
Spain

Monika Rogowska-Stangret
Warsaw University
Poland

Waltraud Ernst
Johannes Kepler University Linz
Austria

Editorial Office
MDPI
St. Alban-Anlage 66
4052 Basel, Switzerland

This is a reprint of articles from the Special Issue published online in the open access journal *Social Sciences* (ISSN 2076-0760) in 2019 (available at: https://www.mdpi.com/journal/socsci/special_issues/Feminist_new_materialsms).

For citation purposes, cite each article independently as indicated on the article page online and as indicated below:

LastName, A.A.; LastName, B.B.; LastName, C.C. Article Title. *Journal Name* **Year**, *Article Number*, Page Range.

ISBN 978-3-03921-808-0 (Pbk)
ISBN 978-3-03921-809-7 (PDF)

© 2020 by the authors. Articles in this book are Open Access and distributed under the Creative Commons Attribution (CC BY) license, which allows users to download, copy and build upon published articles, as long as the author and publisher are properly credited, which ensures maximum dissemination and a wider impact of our publications.

The book as a whole is distributed by MDPI under the terms and conditions of the Creative Commons license CC BY-NC-ND.

Contents

About the Special Issue Editors vii

Beatriz Revelles-Benavente, Waltraud Ernst and Monika Rogowska-Stangret
Feminist New Materialisms: Activating Ethico-Politics through Genealogies in Social Sciences
Reprinted from: *Social Sciences* **2019**, *8*, 296, doi:10.3390/socsci8110296 1

Orianna Calderon-Sandoval and Adelina Sanchez-Espinosa
Feminist Documentary Cinema as a Diffraction Apparatus: A Diffractive Reading of the Spanish Films, *Cuidado, resbala* and *Yes, We Fuck!*
Reprinted from: *Social Sciences* **2019**, *8*, 206, doi:10.3390/socsci8070206 7

Juliana España Keller
The Sonic Intra-Face of a Noisy Feminist Social Kitchen
Reprinted from: *Social Sciences* **2019**, *8*, 245, doi:10.3390/socsci8090245 21

Anna Hickey-Moody and Marissa Willcox
Entanglements of Difference as Community Togetherness: Faith, Art and Feminism
Reprinted from: *Social Sciences* **2019**, *8*, 264, doi:10.3390/socsci8090264 43

Suvi Pihkala, Tuija Huuki and Vappu Sunnari
Moving with Touch: Entanglements of a Child, Valentine's Day Cards, and Research–Activism against Sexual Harassment in Pre-Teen Peer Cultures
Reprinted from: *Social Sciences* **2019**, *8*, 226, doi:10.3390/socsci8080226 64

Miranda Imperial
New Materialist Feminist Ecological Practices: La Via Campesina and Activist Environmental Work
Reprinted from: *Social Sciences* **2019**, *8*, 235, doi:10.3390/socsci8080235 77

Tanja Kubes
New Materialist Perspectives on Sex Robots. A Feminist Dystopia/Utopia?
Reprinted from: *Social Sciences* **2019**, *8*, 224, doi:10.3390/socsci8080224 92

About the Special Issue Editors

Beatriz Revelles-Benavente is a lecturer at the University of Granada, at the Department of English Language and Literature. She is also the co-editor of the journal Matter: Journal of New Materialist Research, as well as one of the Spanish management committee in the COST Action IS1307: Networking European New Materialisms: How matter comes to matter. Additionally, she has organized the V New Materialist Conference at the Universitat Oberta de Catalunya and the IV Training School on New Materialisms at the University of Barcelona. Furthermore, she is the co-editor of the book published by Routledge Teaching Gender: Feminist Pedagogy and Responsability in Times of Political Crisis. Currently, her lines of research are concerned with the connection between literature and society via social media and the like economy using both a feminist and a new materialist lens.

Monika Rogowska-Stangret is a postdoctoral researcher in the fields of feminist philosophy, gender studies and posthumanism. She teaches at the Institute of Philosophy, Warsaw University and at the Polish-Japanese Academy of Information Technology in Warsaw. She was a member of the Management Committee in the European project New Materialism: Networking European Scholarship on 'How Matter Comes to Matter', European Cooperation in Science and Technology (COST), Action IS 1307 (2013–2018) and is now engaged in creating a new journal: Matter: Journal of New Materialist Research as a co-editor of a section "Praxiography*: Practices and Institutions". She organized the 7th Annual Conference on the New Materialisms: Performing Situated Knowledges: Space, Time, Vulnerability, 21–23.09.2016, Institute of Philosophy and Sociology, Polish Academy of Sciences, Warsaw. More info: https://independent.academia.edu/MonikaRogowskaStangret.

Waltraud Ernst (PhD) is a philosopher and senior researcher at the Institute for Women's and Gender Studies, Johannes Kepler University Linz, Austria. She served as Austrian MC member of the EU COST Action IS 1307 New Materialism. Networking European Scholarship on, "How matter comes to matter". In 2018 she was a visiting professor for Gender and Diversity perspectives in Engineering at the Technical University of Dresden. Her research interests cover the history and future of gender in technosciences as well as feminist epistemology and ethics & politics of globalization. Recently published: Emancipatory Interferences with Machines? http://genderandset.open.ac.uk/index.php/genderandset/article/view/509 and Gender in Science and Technology http://e-book.fwf.ac.at/o:453.

Editorial

Feminist New Materialisms: Activating Ethico-Politics through Genealogies in Social Sciences

Beatriz Revelles-Benavente [1,*], Waltraud Ernst [2] and Monika Rogowska-Stangret [3,4]

1. Department of English and German Philology, Faculty of Philosophy and Letters, University of Granada, 18071 Granada, Spain
2. Institute of Women's and Gender Studies, Johannes Kepler University Linz, 4040 Linz, Austria; waltraud.ernst@jku.at
3. Institute of Philosophy, University of Warsaw, 00-927 Warsaw, Poland; monika.rogowska@gmail.com
4. Department of New Media Arts, Polish-Japanese Academy of Information Technology, 02-008 Warsaw, Poland
* Correspondence: beatrizrevelles@ugr.es

Received: 21 October 2019; Accepted: 21 October 2019; Published: 23 October 2019

The idea to create a Special Issue journal around the topic of feminist new materialisms emerged out of the editors' collaboration in the frames of European project *New Materialism: Networking European Scholarship on 'How Matter Comes to Matter'* (European Cooperation in Science and Technology), and more specifically it was born at the 9th Annual Conference on the New Materialisms, held at Utrecht University in June 2018. The editors were then able to trace the discussions within new materialism, but also on the margins of it, and in dialogues with researchers with different academic backgrounds or coming from other theoretical standpoints. Those dialogues all have different affective modalities, raised various theoretical (counter) arguments, and imagined heterogeneous practices. As editors of this issue of "Social Sciences," we recognized the need to rethink feminist new materialisms, yet again accentuating and activating its ethico-political dimensions and stakes. We are undertaking this endeavour together with scholars, who have been composing the cartography of feminist new materialist research for some time now (among them: Alaimo and Hekman 2008; Coole and Frost 2010; Dolphijn and van der Tuin 2012; Van der Tuin 2015; Cielemęcka and Rogowska-Stangret 2018), and we aim at grasping specifically its ethico-political practices.

For us, new materialisms have always been the entanglement of epistemology, ontology, ethics, and politics. Looking back to the notion of "situated knowledges" by Haraway (1988) who—among others—"planted the seed for feminist new materialism" (Van der Tuin 2015, p. 26)—one sees how those (at least) four planes are entangled (Rogowska-Stangret 2018), in order to bring forth "response-able" (Haraway 2008) research. New materialism is thus an ethico-onto-epistemological framework (Barad 2007; Revelles-Benavente 2018), that by activating its ethico-politics helps to diagnose, infer, and transform gendered, environmental, anthropocentric, and social injustices from a multidimensional angle. Social injustices are a driving motivation to pursue research, and are the reason why the editors and authors of this special issue cannot understand new materialism without feminism (Hinton and Treusch 2015; Ernst 2016). Contemporary feminist researchers are providing new materialisms with a transversal approach (Yuval-Davis 1997) that comes from many different disciplines, without canonizing back again knowledge creation and production, and in hope that they will not enter back into classifixations (Van der Tuin 2015). It is a "situated" (Haraway 1988) research "response-able" (Haraway 2008) to material-discursive practices that iterate in a dynamic conceptualization of matter.

The authors of this issue aim at adding to the body of research which relates with methodologies and empirical work in new materialism (e.g., Fox and Allred 2015; Tamboukou 2015; De Freitas and Palmer 2016). Following Fox and Allred (2015) guidelines, the authors reflect upon the differences that using this methodology has provided to the research itself. We believe in a relational conceptualization of bodies and objects, and the importance of affect in this relation; while instead of territorializing and deterritorializing the performed research, we focus on the processes that iterate the research through "queering linearity" (Barad 2010).

We argue that methodology necessarily needs to engage within the relation between acting and thinking (Tamboukou 2015), so that it can transform itself into a political practice embodied and embedded. Experimenting with the linearity of the process provides the actualization of future becomings and because of that, the materialization of agential practices while they are occurring. As a conclusion, we will focus on the necessity to think of methodology, ontology, ethics, politics, and epistemology as a processual relation, and the need to focus on processes instead of results (Grosz 2005) for a feminist politics of affinities instead of identities.

1. Putting the Ethico-Political Back to Research

New materialisms refer to a specific ethico-political and onto-epistemological turn that is deeply committed to de-centralizing knowledge production, cutting across pre-established dichotomies, and focusing on processes transversing hierarchies of power relations that organize diverse forms of life. In particular, it is a methodology of situating material-discursive practices that form specific socio-cultural phenomena via a relational ontology. Here, different elements come to being through intra-actions. Agency materializes and redefines itself as a more than isolated human agency. New materialist approaches to the creation and dissemination of scientific knowledge are proliferating across diverse disciplines such as arts (e.g., Kontturi et al. 2018; Barrett et al. 2017; Barrett and Bolt 2013), science and technology (e.g., Ernst et al. 2017), contemporary philosophy (e.g., Cielemęcka and Rogowska-Stangret 2018; Bühlmann et al. 2017; Revelles-Benavente et al. 2014; Dolphijn and van der Tuin 2012; Coole and Frost 2010), cultural and media studies (e.g., Tiainen et al. 2015), and social sciences (e.g., Juelskjær et al.; Bath et al. 2017; Fox and Allred 2017; Alaimo and Hekman 2008). Although in the mentioned publications the ethico-political frames are strongly present, this is not the case for how new materialisms are recognized and represented in academia in general. Often, the more recognition new materialisms get in academia, the less space and time is devoted to their ethico-political frames. As a result, the feminist, queer, postcolonial, and ecological stakes are given less attention and importance; and the ethico-political frames of feminist new materialisms are amputated from the onto-epistemological turn. In this present issue of "Social Sciences," the authors and editors are committed to stressing the importance of ethico-political frames to feminist new materialisms.

According to Dolphijn and van der Tuin (2012), new materialisms are about putting them to work, which means that it is not to be described, but performed. The authors and editors of this issue add yet another loop that has to do with situating new materialisms as ethico-politics. We would like to put new materialisms to work for feminist, queer, postcolonial, and ecological practices. The papers invite us to understand feminism with new materialisms and vice-versa. Our approach to this field of research is strongly marked by the concepts of genealogies (Van der Tuin 2015), feminicity (Colman 2014), diffracting diffraction (Barad 2014), and the processes of becoming and sense-making of our own flexible and multiple identities (Braidotti 2013). That is, our approach has to do with how we build, contemporaneously, our epistemological genealogies effectively to produce points of activation for feminist, queer, postcolonial, and ecological practices. We present examples which investigate new social bondings and community building beyond identity politics, and contributions dealing with specific instances of realities that engage with the world with an entanglement between feminist ethics, politics, and methodologies.

2. Putting New Materialisms to Work

This special issue assembles perspectives from a wide range of disciplinary fields such as film studies, sound and noise art, arts-based community research and education, feminist environmentalism and ecology, as well as diffractive design and human-machine interaction. The six research papers allow insight into diverse areas such as feminist documentary cinema, participatory practices in performance artwork, feminist and intra-religious collaborative art practices and Instagram-based art communities, creative workshops addressing sexual harassment in pre-teen peer cultures, feminist ecological practices and activist environmental work in Brazil, as well as the vision of robot sex beyond fixed human-centered heteronormalizations. The authors come not only from different academic disciplines but also from different national and transnational positionings such as Spain, Australia, Germany, Finland, and the UK. These investigations are connected in a very systematic, yet colorful way, through their theoretical and methodological foundation in feminist new materialism which proves, on this way, to be traveling in many parts of the intellectual world. The papers are also connected via an ethico-onto-epistemological commitment to not only scrutinize oppression and conflict, but also work for transforming our social and cultural imaginations through enacting or putting to work ideas, materialities, and lived realities that are founded in feminist, queer, postcolonial, and ecological practices. The papers show how it is possible to analyze these practices as becoming real, and as moments or processes of materialization.

The article "Feminist Documentary Cinema as Diffraction Apparatus: A Diffracting Reading of the Spanish Films, *Cuidado, Resbala* and *Yes, We Fuck!*" by Orianna Calderon-Sandoval and Adelina Sánchez-Espinosa, use "materiality, emotionality, and performativity" (p. 7) as analytical tools to render visible the potential of feminist documentary cinema for building alliances from and against precarity. It is done through close-watching of two Spanish films *Cuidado, Resbala* and *Yes, We Fuck!* on domestic workers, and sexually and functionally diverse communities. The authors show how the films operate as feminist countervisuality devices that reframe realities, and open up possibilities for being, becoming, and imagining the worlds otherwise—outside of androcentric paradigms. (Calderon-Sandoval and Sanchez-Espinosa 2019).

Juliana España Keller in her "The Sonic Intra-Face of a Noisy Feminist Social Kitchen," shows how the reframing of the kitchen table into a platform for "exploring, repositioning and amplifying kitchen tools as material phenomena through electronic and manual manipulation into an immersive sonic performance installation" (p. 21) can contribute to "forming daring dissonant narratives that feed post-human ethical practices and feminist genealogies" (p. 21). By using and analyzing participatory practices in performance art, the kitchen becomes a noisy, social kitchen through collaborative engagements of more than human contributors. The author argues for a noisy culture of social reimagining of the kitchen through somatic learning in performative art practices. (España Keller 2019).

Anna Hickey-Moody and Marissa Willcox, in the article "Entanglements of Difference as Community Togetherness: Faith, Art and Feminism," are also exploring collaborative art practices, here in creative workshops with children in intra-religious communities, with different ethnic backgrounds, and in presenting and analyzing a broadcasted live-interview in an Instagram-based feminist art community. However here, the focus lies on enacting new ways of feelings of belonging, and building community beyond sameness. The authors offer a diffraction of differences, that through research understood as being-with, results in the emerging of "togetherness" as "collections of difference" (Hickey-Moody and Willcox 2019, p. 61).

The article, "Moving with Touch: Entanglements of a Child, Valentine's Day Cards, and Research-Activism against Sexual Harassment in Pre-Teen Peer Cultures," by Suvi Pihkala, Tuija Huuki, and Vappu Sunnari, undertakes the question of sexual violence in pre-teen peer cultures as a response to discussions around the "#MeToo" movement, in which sexual harassment in children's environments was neglected to a great extent. Through exploring "microprocesses of change within the more-than-human child-card entanglements" (p. 64), the authors present and analyze the "affective charge in moments and movements of response and resistance" (p. 64) in workshops with children. In particular, they concentrate on touch and its different affective, sensing, and material effects, in hope to bring forth ways to enable "recognition, response, and resistance" (p. 64). (Suvi Pihkala and Sunnari 2019).

Miranda Imperial in "New Materialist Feminist Ecological Practices: La Via Campesina and Activist Environmental Work," presents a relocation of the grassroots activism of the women's section of the famous

Brazilian self-organization of peasants, La Via Campesina, within the genealogies of ecological feminism and new materialist environmentalisms. The author delves into three examples of how in the recent past, feminist Indigenous activists successfully opposed multinational agrobusinesses, genetically modified crops, and land-grabbing practices. Imperial calls for collective action, and transnational community building for "re-distributing, re-thinking, and responding to the planet." (Imperial 2019, p. 87).

The article, "New Materialist Perspectives on Sex Robots. A Feminist Dystopia/Utopia?" by Tanja Kubes, presents sex robots as potential agencies in the becoming of human-machine-entanglements which serve to redefine robot sex as "refutation of normative definitions of sex" (Kubes 2019, p. 224). The author discusses the status quo of the development of the so-called sex robots, as well as arguments which turn against this endeavor because of the fact that "prototypes of sex robots aiming to hit the market in the near future are definitely hinting towards a questionable understanding of ideals of female beauty, and the nature of gender relations" (Kubes 2019, p. 92). The paper explores the potential of sex robotics for "leaving the beaten track of pornographic mimicry and sexist hyperfeminization" (Kubes 2019, p. 101), and contributing instead to "new forms of sexual pleasure beyond fixed heteronormative normalizations" (Kubes 2019, p. 101).

3. Actualizing Future Becomings

The articles gathered in this issue of "Social Sciences" are putting new materialisms to work through diverse methodologies, mobilizing a variety of research backgrounds, contexts, and topics. They offer affective relational conceptualizations of bodies as they co-emerge together with films, sounds, creative workshops, live-interviews, experiences of touch (in its ambiguity), environmental and feminist activism and sex technologies, and try to grasp the specificities and effects of these relationalities. They are acting and thinking, doing and conceptualizing, providing at the same time joy, energy, concern, and care, to experiment, imagine, and design ways of doing and thinking. They activate ethico-political dimensions of feminist new materialisms through research, and activist efforts to transform social, environmental, gendered, and anthropocentric injustices, and to think of recognition of those injustices, resistance, and responses to them. By doing that, they also struggle to bring forth the future dimension of the research undertaken, to actualize future becomings, bodies, communities, responses, affinities, ways of sensing-feeling, bringing together, and experiencing. They prove the fact that feminist new materialist research is an open-ended process that directs us to yet new questions, horizons, and conceptualizations; enlivens our imagination and the desire to experiment with concepts and practices; and re-imagine and re-design oppressive and unjust paradigms.

Funding: This research was funded by EU COST Action IS 1307 *New Materialism. Networking European Scholarship on 'How matter comes to matter'*. Monika Rogowska-Stangret's contribution was funded by the grant from the Ministry of Science and Higher Education in Poland in the frames of the "National Program for the Development of the Humanities" (2016–2019).

Conflicts of Interest: The authors declare no conflict of interest.

References

Alaimo, Stacy, and Susan Hekman. 2008. *Material Feminisms*. Bloomington: Indiana University Press.
Barad, Karen. 2007. *Meeting the Universe Halfway: Quantum Physics and the Entanglement of Matter and Meaning*. Durham: Duke University Press.
Barad, Karen. 2010. Quantum Entanglements and Hauntological Relations of Inheritance: Dis/continuities, SpaceTime Enfoldings, and Justice-to-Come. *Derrida Today* 3: 240–68. [CrossRef]
Barad, Karen. 2014. Diffracting Diffraction: Cutting Together-Apart. *Parallax* 20: 168–87. [CrossRef]
Barrett, Estelle, and Barbara Bolt. 2013. *Carnal Knowledge: Towards a "New Materialism" Through The Arts*. London and New York: I.B.Tauris.
Barrett, Estelle, Barbara Bolt, and Kontturi Katve-Kaisa. 2017. Studies in Material Thinking, 16. Available online: https://www.materialthinking.org/volumes/volume-16 (accessed on 22 October 2019).

Bath, Corinna, Hanna Meißner, Stephan Trinkaus, and Susanne Völker. 2017. *Verantwortung und Un/Verfügbarkeit. Impulse und Zugänge eines (neo)materialistischen Feminismus*. Münster: Westfälisches Dampfboot. (In German)

Braidotti, Rosi. 2013. *The Posthuman*. Cambridge and Malden: Polity Press.

Bühlmann, Vera, Felicity Colman, and Iris van der Tuin. 2017. Introduction to new materialist genealogies: New matelialisms, novel mentalities, quantum literacy. *Minnesota Review* 88: 47–58. [CrossRef]

Calderon-Sandoval, Orianna, and Adelina Sanchez-Espinosa. 2019. Feminist Documentary Cinema as a Diffraction Apparatus: A Diffractive Reading of the Spanish Films, *Cuidado, resbala* and *Yes, We Fuck! Social Sciences* 8: 206. [CrossRef]

Cielemęcka, Olga, and Monika Rogowska-Stangret. 2018. Feministyczne nowe materializmy: Usytuowane kartografie. Lublin: e-naukowiec. Available online: http://e-naukowiec.eu/wp-content/uploads/2018/05/ksi%C4%85%C5%BCka-wersja-ostateczna-2.pdf (accessed on 22 October 2019).

Colman, Felicity. 2014. Digital feminicity: Predication and measurement, materialist informatics and images. In *New Feminist Materialism. Engendering an Ethic-onto-Epistemological Methodology*. Edited by Beatriz Revelles-Benavente, Ana M. González and Krizia Nardini. Barcelona: Artnodes. [CrossRef]

Coole, Diana, and Samantha Frost. 2010. *New Materialisms: Ontology, Agency, and Politics*. Durham: Duke University Press.

De Freitas, Elizabeth, and Helen Palmer. 2016. How scientific concepts come to matter in early childhood curriculum: Rethinking the concept of force. *Cultural Studies of Science Education* 11: 1201–22. [CrossRef]

Dolphijn, Rick, and Iris van der Tuin. 2012. *New Materialism: Interviews & Cartographies*. Ann Arbor: Open Humanities Press.

Ernst, Waltraud. 2016. In connection: Feminist Epistemology for the Twenty-first Century. *Transcultural Studies* 12: 267–87. [CrossRef]

Ernst, Waltraud, Corinna Bath, and Marja Vehviläinen. 2017. Special Issue: Political Objects—Prescriptions. Injustices and Promises of Material Agents. *International Journal of Gender, Science and Technology* 9. Available online: http://genderandset.open.ac.uk/index.php/genderandset/issue/view/27 (accessed on 22 October 2019).

España Keller, Juliana. 2019. The Sonic Intra-Face of a Noisy Feminist Social Kitchen. *Social Sciences* 8: 245. [CrossRef]

Fox, Nick, and Pam Allred. 2015. New materialist social inquiry: designs, methods and the research-assemblage. *International Journal of Social Research Methodology* 18: 399–414. [CrossRef]

Fox, Nick, and Pam Allred. 2017. *Sociology and the New Materialism: Theory, Research, Action*. London: SAGE Publications.

Grosz, Elizabeth. 2005. *Time Travels: Feminism, Nature, Power*. Durham: Duke University Press.

Haraway, Donna. 1988. Situated Knowledges: The Science Question in Feminism and the Privilege of Partial Perspective. *Feminist Studies* 14: 575–99. [CrossRef]

Haraway, Donna. 2008. *When Species Meet*. Minneapolis and London: University of Minnesota Press.

Hickey-Moody, Anna, and Marissa Willcox. 2019. Entanglements of Difference as Community Togetherness: Faith, Art and Feminism. *Social Sciences* 8: 264. [CrossRef]

Hinton, Peta, and Pat Treusch. 2015. *Teaching with Feminist Materialisms*. Utrecht: Atgender.

Imperial, Miranda. 2019. New Materialist Feminist Ecological Practices: La Via Campesina and Activist Environmental Work. *Social Sciences* 8: 235. [CrossRef]

Juelskjær, Malou, Helle Plauborg, and Adrian Stine Willum. Forthcoming. *Dialogues on Agential Realism—Engaging in Worldings*. New York: Routledge.

Kontturi, Katve-Kaisa, Milla Tiainen, Tero Nauha, and Marie-Luise Angerer. 2018. Aesthetic Intra-Actions. Practising New Materialisms in the Art. 2018, Ruukku: Studies in Artistic Research, SAR (Society for Artistic Research): Available online: http://ruukku-journal.fi/en/issues/9 (accessed on 22 October 2019).

Kubes, Tanja. 2019. New Materialist Perspectives on Sex Robots. A Feminist Dystopia/Utopia? *Social Sciences* 8: 224. [CrossRef]

Suvi Pihkala, Huuki Tuija Suvi, and Vappu Sunnari. 2019. Moving with Touch: Entanglements of a Child, Valentine's Day Cards, and Research—Activism against Sexual Harassment in Pre-Teen Peer Cultures. *Social Sciences* 8: 226. [CrossRef]

Revelles-Benavente, Beatriz. 2018. Material knowledges: Intra-acting van der Tuin's new materialism with Barad's agential realism. Enrahonar. *An International Journal of Theoretical and Practical Reason* 60: 75–91. [CrossRef]

Revelles-Benavente, Beatriz, Ana M. González, and Krizia Nardini. 2014. Nuevo materialismo feminista: engendrar una metodología ético-onto-epistemológica. *Artnodes* 14. (In Spanish). [CrossRef]

Rogowska-Stangret, Monika. 2018. Situated Knowledges. *The New Materialist Almanac*. Edited by David Gauthier and Sam Skinner. Available online: http://newmaterialism.eu/almanac/s/situated-knowledges.html (accessed on 22 October 2019).

Tamboukou, Maria. 2015. Narrative phenomena: Entanglements and intra-actions in narrative research. In *Discourse and narrative methods: Theoretical Departures, Analytical Strategies and Situated Writings*. Edited by Mona Livholts and Maria Tamboukou. London: SAGE Publications, pp. 37–47.

Tiainen, Milla, Kontturi Katve-Kaisa, and Ilona Hongisto. 2015. Movement, Aesthetics, Ontology. *Cultural Studies Review* 21: 4–13.

Van der Tuin, Iris. 2015. *Generational Feminism. New Materialist Introduction to a Generative Approach*. London: Lexington Books.

Yuval-Davis, Nira. 1997. *Gender and Nation*. London: SAGE Publications.

© 2019 by the authors. Licensee MDPI, Basel, Switzerland. This article is an open access article distributed under the terms and conditions of the Creative Commons Attribution (CC BY) license (http://creativecommons.org/licenses/by/4.0/).

Article

Feminist Documentary Cinema as a Diffraction Apparatus: A Diffractive Reading of the Spanish Films, *Cuidado, resbala* and *Yes, We Fuck!*

Orianna Calderon-Sandoval *[ID] and Adelina Sanchez-Espinosa[ID]

Research Centre for Women's and Gender Studies, University of Granada, 18071 Granada, Spain
* Correspondence: orianna@correo.ugr.es

Received: 25 April 2019; Accepted: 27 June 2019; Published: 2 July 2019

Abstract: Following Karen Barad's diffractive methodology, we encounter feminist documentary cinema as a diffraction apparatus: that is, as technologies that make part of the world intelligible to another part of the world in specific ways, by means of intra-actions between human and non-human agencies and objects of observation. We propose three analytical tools: materiality, emotionality, and performativity. In this article, we analyse two Spanish documentary films that render visible the potential of feminist documentary cinema for building alliances from and against precarity: *Cuidado, resbala* and *Yes, We Fuck!* Reading the insights and patterns raised in each case study through one another (i.e., diffractively), we discuss the intra-actions by which each of these films participates in co-creating the real. We end up describing three possible effects of feminist material-discursive practices in documentary cinema.

Keywords: Documentary; diffraction apparatus; diffractive reading; *Cuidado, resbala*; *Yes, We Fuck!*; Spanish cinema; materiality; emotionality; performativity

---

1. Introduction

This article explores Karen Barad's diffractive methodology (Barad 2007) as a bridge between feminist documentary cinema and new materialist perspectives.[1] We argue that feminist documentary films can be productively encountered as diffraction apparatuses: that is, as technologies that make part of the world intelligible to another part of the world in specific ways, by means of intra-actions between human and non-human agencies and objects of observation.

As a visualisation metaphor opposed to reflection, diffraction changes the focus from mirroring and sameness to attending "patterns of difference" (Barad 2007, p. 29), and "effects of difference" (Haraway [1992] 2004, p. 70). Such an onto-epistemological turn has ethico-political effects, as it moves from "reflecting on representations" to "accounting for how practices matter" (Barad 2007, p. 90). Moving away from the representational paradigm in the analysis of documentary cinema has an ethical impact, changing the focus "from producing accurate and authentic representations to creatively contributing to the transformability of actual beings in the real" (Hongisto 2015, p. 12).[2]

---

[1] In her PhD thesis, co-supervised by Adelina Sánchez-Espinosa, Beatriz Revelles's employs diffractive methodology as a bridge between the Social Sciences and the Humanities (Revelles Benavente 2014, p. 75). Our article takes its inspiration from this proposal.

[2] For a comprehensive revision of the concept of social representation, see Rubira García et al. (2018). It could be productive to read Barad's diffractive methodology through Serge Moscovici's theory of social representations, particularly due to his understanding of representation not as reproduction, but as a re-production, i.e., a new production of meaning "born from the interactions between the subjects (at all levels, including individual, group, institution, or at a massive scale) and the object itself" (Rubira García et al. 2018, p. 3). His approach blurs the separation between object and subject, focusing instead on the interactions which, for Barad, are more accurately described as intra-actions, as explained in the next section. Like

Most of the first independent films made by feminist activists in the seventies belong to the realist documentary film tradition.[3] Documentaries such as Union Maids (Union Maids 1976) showed the lives of women outside the limited range of female images in classical cinema, which supports the argument that they displayed more "accurate" realities. However, feminist theorists like Claire Johnston soon began to challenge realistic aesthetics. She argues that realism maintains the delusion of classical cinema by pretending the non-intervention of the filmmakers limited, apparently, to showing reality as it is. The gaze of the camera is supposed to be innocent:

> What the camera in fact grasps is the "natural" world of the dominant ideology. Women's cinema cannot afford such idealism; the "truth" of our oppression cannot be "captured" on celluloid with the "innocence" of the camera: it has to be constructed/manufactured. New meanings have to be created by disrupting the fabric of the male bourgeois cinema within the text of the film. (Johnston [1973] 2000, p. 29)

The clash of these two positions, realist documentary vs. counter-cinema[4], leads to the so-called realist debate of the late seventies. Within feminist film theory, the debate increasingly begins to be in favour of anti-realism, thus distinguishing two successive moments in feminist film production: Firstly, an effort to change the content of dominant cinema, by means of portraying women talking about their "real" experiences; secondly, a growing interest in film form. Nevertheless, theorists such as Julia Lesage have refused the sharp rejection of cinematic realism and have questioned this apparent succession. The production of realist feminist documentaries has continued alongside more risky formal experiments, so that "both realist and experimental documentary forms have been politicized by feminist filmmakers" (Lesage 1984, p. 246).

We argue that the diffraction metaphor can move this debate forward by accounting for how material-discursive practices in feminist filmmaking matter. We agree with Ilona Hongisto's affirmation that "documentaries do not only operate on a plane of signification, but also partake in the material processes that co-compose the real" (Hongisto 2015, p. 12). For her, the main way in which politically committed documentary films participate in "the real as process" (Hongisto 2015, p. 12) is through framing, which involves making cuts and drawing boundaries within phenomena. That is also what diffraction apparatuses do.

This article is divided into four sections. The first section introduces diffractive methodology as a reading strategy and as a visualisation metaphor and develops our conceptualisation of feminist documentary cinema as a diffraction apparatus. In the second section, we discuss the potential of feminist documentary cinema for building alliances from and against precarity, the framework in which we locate our two case studies, i.e., Spanish documentary films *Cuidado, resbala* (2013) and *Yes, We Fuck!* (2015). These are diffractively read in the third section. In the last section, we describe three possible effects of feminist material-discursive practices in documentary cinema by reading through one another (i.e., diffractively) insights and patterns raised in each case study.

Barad, Moscovici resorts to quantum-physics inspired metaphors to explain the active role of representations in co-creating the real: "Here and there we find a tendency to consider that social representations are the inner reflection of something external, the surface and ephemeral layer of something deeper and more permanent. While everything points to see in them a constitutive factor of social reality, just as invisible particles and fields are a constitutive factor of physical reality" (Rubira Garcia et al. 2018, p. 3).

[3] Realism in cinema is characterised by representations that "present an appearance of transparency by effacing the processes of meaning production in their own textual operations." (Kuhn 1994, p. 151).

[4] Peter Wollen coined the term "counter-cinema" in 1972. The features of this type of cinema are, according to Wollen, those that oppose the characteristics of mainstream Hollywood productions, namely, "estrangement", "narrative intransitivity", "aperture" and "unpleasure", among others (Wollen [1972] 2002). It is a year after, in 1973 that Claire Johnston talks about feminist cinema in terms of counter-cinema.

2. From the Reflecting Mirror to the Diffraction Apparatus

Diffraction is a concept used in physics to describe wave behaviour. As a quantum phenomenon, diffraction broke the paradigms of classical physics, since the double slit experiment[5] proved that "the ontology of anything cannot be determined without regard to the apparatus of observation, or else that the apparatus participates in the ontology of the thing observed" (Belia 2015, p. 14).

In feminist theory, the metaphor of diffraction is employed to describe a critical consciousness that is attentive to differences and their effects. Donna Haraway asks us to consider what the physical phenomenon of diffraction could mean in onto-epistemological terms. She explains that, as a metaphor, diffraction "drops the metaphysics of identity and the metaphysics of representation and says optics is full of a whole other potent way of thinking about light, which is about history. It's not about identity as taxonomy, but it's about registering process on the recording screen" (Haraway 2000, pp. 103–4).

In accordance with this perspective, a documentary film would not be conceived as the reflection of any so-called fixed reality out there, which is then mirrored by the camera. Instead, it is analysed as technologies that co-produce and record the processes through which human elements (e.g., the filmmakers) and non-human elements (e.g., the camera) intra-act with other human and non-human parts of the world (e.g., filmed subjects and objects, spectators, screens).

Apart from the optical metaphor, Barad also employs diffraction to describe a reading methodology that attends to "entanglements in reading important insights and approaches through one another" (Barad 2007, p. 30). Within a diffractive approach, "any reading of texts is a meaning-making practice" (Belia 2015, p. 16). Rather than focus on accurate reflections of the world, diffractive reading engages in the re-making of the world. Birgit Kaiser defines diffractive reading as "radically performative" (Kaiser 2014, p. 281): it is by reading texts together that certain patterns emerge, so that reading in itself becomes a productive event.

The separation between subject/observer and object/observed is replaced by an understanding that both are permanently entangled. Diffraction does not take the boundaries of any subject nor object for granted, "but rather investigates the material-discursive boundary-making practices that produce 'objects' and 'subjects' and other differences out of, and in terms of, a changing relationality" (Barad 2007, p. 93). Rather than "interactions", Barad talks about "intra-actions" to highlight the fact that objects and agencies of observation are mutually constituted in their encounters.

To conceive feminist documentary films as diffraction apparatuses that "enact what matters and what is excluded from mattering" (Barad 2007, p. 148) from a gender-aware perspective involves analysing how the films intra-act with different parts of the world, the differences they make, and where the effects of those differences appear. This means reading them as entangled with their filmmakers' positions, the production decisions surrounding them, and their reception effects.

We propose three tools for analysing documentary cinema as a diffraction apparatus: materiality, emotionality and performativity. Materiality is a term borrowed from Domitilla Olivieri's PhD thesis, in which she uses the expression "materiality of documentary" to describe two aspects. Firstly, she argues for "the filmic representation in its material specificity" (Olivieri 2012, p. 42), which involves going beyond the content (i.e., narrative structures, plot and subject matter), and paying attention to "how the film is constructed: its technologies, framing, editing, voice-over, use of realistic or fictional images and sounds, and use of different filmic strategies" (Olivieri 2012, p. 10). Secondly, materiality "refers to the manner in which documentary film engages with bodies and with the matter of the world" (Olivieri 2012, p. 10).

---

[5] Thomas Young performed the double-slit experiment with light in 1801. In 1927, Davisson and Germer demonstrated that electrons show the same behaviour: "The Davisson-Germer experiment showed that under some circumstances, matter (in this case electrons) exhibits wavelike behavior. Since the Davisson and Germer experiment, many other experiments have confirmed this result for other kinds of matter as well. That is, there is direct empirical evidence that matter—not just light—manifests wave behavior under the right experimental circumstances." (Barad 2007, p. 83).

The second tool, performativity, is understood in four senses following Nichols (2010); Bruzzi (2000); Butler (1990, 2015) and Barad (2007). For Bill Nichols, the performative is one of the six possible modes of representation in documentary cinema.[6] This mode emphasises the subjective dimensions of our knowledge of the world by stressing "the emotional complexity of experience from the perspective of the filmmaker him- or herself" (Nichols 2010, p. 202). Information and facts yield to "an expressive quality that affirms the highly situated, embodied, and vividly personal perspective of specific subjects" (Nichols 2010, p. 203). It is less concerned with formal experimentation in itself and, despite the centrality it gives to personal experience, it always joins "the particular to the general, the individual to the collective, and the personal to the political" (Nichols 2010, p. 204).

Some critics, however, claim that documentary cinema is always a performative act, regardless of its mode of representation. Stella Bruzzi, for instance, argues that documentaries are "the result of the intrusion of the filmmaker onto the situation being filmed" (Bruzzi 2000, p. 8). This, she continues, does not invalidate the authenticity of documentary. Rather, in her opinion, the idea of unmediated transparency is replaced "with a performative exchange between subjects, filmmakers/apparatus and spectators" (Bruzzi 2000, p. 6). Instead of presenting a reality that exists previously and independently, performative documentary cinema shows realities resulting from the intervention of the camera and/or the film production, situations created from the very action of making a documentary film. This definition of documentary as a performative act that captures some sort of reality in-the-making echoes Barad's understanding of reality as "an ongoing dynamic of intra-activity" (Barad 2007, p. 206).

Judith Butler first looked at the concept of performativity through feminist lenses in her 1990 book *Gender Trouble. Feminism and the Subversion of identity*. The concept of performativity originally refers to linguistic utterances that bring what they state into being or make a set of events happen as a consequence of the utterance being made. In Butler's words: "performativity is a way of naming a power language has to bring about a new situation or to set into motion a set of effects" (Butler 2015, p. 28). Paraphrasing her, we would like to propose performativity as a way of naming the power of documentary cinema "to bring about a new situation or to set into motion a set of effects" (Butler 2015, p. 28).

A new materialist reading of Butler's performativity has been elaborated by Mónica Cano (Cano Abadía 2017). She argues that Butler replaces the humanist subject with a vulnerable, interdependent subject who is open to change and to the constitutive relationship with others (Cano Abadía 2017, p. 266). We agree with her on this aspect, which is further developed in the next section. Cano also states that Butler does not reduce matter to language, nor does she enclose the subjects in a rigid socio-linguistic mechanism that produces them in a deterministic way (Cano Abadía 2017, p. 269).

What we want to emphasise from Barad's take on performativity is precisely the relevance she gives to matter: "an agential realist elaboration of performativity allows matter its due as an active participant in the world's becoming, in its ongoing intra-activity" (Barad 2007, p. 136). Hence, the performativity of documentary cinema as a diffraction apparatus, which includes human and non-human agents and objects of observation, matters at various levels: from the way it frames and creates boundaries, to the alliances it helps sustain on both sides of the camera and the screen.

Our third tool, emotionality, describes "how texts are 'moving', or how they generate effects (...) [and] the way in which texts name or perform different emotions" (Ahmed 2014, p. 13). Sara Ahmed is explicit about why she decides to employ the word "emotion" rather than "affect": "I was interested in this idea of movement that is explicit in its etymology. And it was also partly that I wanted to use the word that is used in everyday life" (Ahmed 2014, p. 97). She explains the connection between emotions and the making of boundaries:

---

[6] The other modes are: expository, observational, participatory, poetic and reflexive.

> ... it is through emotions, or how we respond to objects and others, that surfaces or boundaries are made: the "I" and the "we" are shaped by, and even take the shape of, contact with others (...) the surfaces of bodies "surface" as an effect of the impressions left by others (...) emotions are not "in" either the individual or the social, but produce the very surfaces and boundaries that allow the individual and the social to be delineated as if they are objects. (Ahmed 2014, p. 10)

In this sense, we look for the emotions evoked by each film: how making and/or watching these films affect(s) subjects and objects on both sides of the camera and the screen. We conceive emotions as "effects rather than origins" (Ahmed 2014, p. 196).

Diffraction, therefore, is a multi-layered concept which we apply in this article in two different manners: one, we argue that any documentary film can be analysed as a diffraction apparatus that makes the world intelligible in specific ways and participates in co-creating the real; two, we diffractively read the insights raised by two case studies so as to identify effects of feminist material-discursive practices in documentary cinema.

3. Feminist Cinema: Visualising Alliances from and against Precarity

It is not our purpose in this article to look for an essentialist and prescriptive definition of what feminist documentary cinema is or should be. Instead, we follow Olivieri's proposal of "studying what makes a documentary feminist in terms of what a documentary does" (Olivieri 2012, p. 7). Therefore, we focus on the actual exploration and construction of contents, textual structures, formal strategies and means of production, distribution and exhibition which reveal a feminist consciousness, i.e., an awareness of the role that gender has (had) in the organisation and legitimisation of social inequalities.

Feminist documentary cinema can be understood as a form of countervisuality[7], balancing between a lived reality of gender inequalities and imagined alternatives to it. The androcentric regime of gender visuality has been built around the subject of humanism: He is the norm according to which the racialised, sexualised and naturalised others are produced (Cano Abadía 2017, p. 265). What Cano explains is that Butler's theory of gender performativity has opened up a different understanding of subjects, starting from the recognition of their fundamentally interdependent and vulnerable condition.

The fact that we have to cohabitate with other humans and non-humans on which our lives depend, should make us "understand a global obligation imposed upon us to find political and economic forms that minimise precarity and establish economic political equality" (Butler 2015, pp. 121–22). Vulnerability is not inherent to a particular group, but unequally distributed as an effect of power relations under specific conditions. When this is not acknowledged, vulnerability can be used by political discourses as a way to produce and naturalise forms of social inequality.

In feminist theory, it has been argued that women face social vulnerability in a disproportionate way. What Butler warns against is the idea that "women have an unchanging and defining vulnerability" (Butler 2015, p. 140). Rather, she underlines that conditions such as poverty and illiteracy faced mainly by women are caused by an unequal distribution of precariousness fostered by gender power relations and lack of adequate socio-political infrastructures. She also states that women are "at once vulnerable and capable of resistance, and that vulnerability and resistance can, and do, and even must happen at the same time" (Butler 2015, p. 141).

To think about inequality in terms of precarity opens up the possibility for strategic alliances among different groups. In Butler's words: "precarity is the rubric that brings together women, queers, transgender people, the poor, the differently abled, and the stateless, but also religious and racial minorities: it is a social and economic condition, but not an identity" (Butler 2015, p. 58). When various minorities, whose alliance potential stems from their shared precarity, assemble in the streets and/or

---

[7] "Countervisuality" is a concept coined by Nicholas Mirzoeff to refer to a resistant vision structured around the tension between the "need to apprehend and counter a real that does exist but should not, and one that should exist but is as yet becoming" (Mirzoeff 2011, p. 477).

appear together in a media platform to demand their rights, they "enact another idea of equality, freedom and justice than the one that they oppose" (Butler 2015, p. 52).

The two documentary films that we have chosen as case studies render visible this kind of alliance. *Cuidado, resbala* is a collective film developed within a feminist economics framework that (re)positions care labour at the centre of the economic activities. *Yes, We Fuck!* is a postporn transfeminist film, which shows sexually explicit images that seek to question mainstream ideals of desirability, as well as sexual practices framed by ableism and heteropatriarchy. In the next section, we apply the previously described tools (materiality, performativity and emotionality) by tracing overlapping waves, patterns of differences and their effects. This is attained by reading the two documentary films through one another. Both films have been cut into four levels: form, content, production and reception. In order to analyse form and content, we carry out a feminist close reading (Lukic and Sánchez-Espinosa 2011). As for production and reception, the methods have been interviews with filmmakers and fieldwork at screenings.

4. A Diffractive Reading of *Cuidado, resbala*[8] and *Yes, We Fuck!*

The title of the 2013 documentary film *Cuidado, resbala* plays with the two meanings of the word "cuidado" in Spanish, so that it can be roughly translated as *Caution/Care Slippery*. It is directed by two psychologists, a pedagogue, a lawyer, a teacher and a filmmaker (María Camacho Gómez, Montserrat Clos Fabuel, Mercedes Cordero Suárez, Vanessa Gómez Martínez, Carolina Suárez Rasmussen and Leonor Jiménez Moreno) from two feminist associations based in Málaga, Spain.

Sexuality and functional diversity[9] are at the core of *Yes We Fuck!*, a postporn documentary film directed by two Spanish cismen[10], Antonio Centeno and Raúl de la Morena. Postporn cinema "uses sexually explicit imagery to contest and complicate dominant representations of gender, sexuality, race, ethnicity, class, ability, age, body type, and other identity markers" (Miller-Young et al. 2013, p. 9). According to Centeno, "what postporn tries to do is to take the visual language of the ordinary porn, which greatly shapes our idea of what sexuality is, and turn it around, politicise it and turn those who were objects into subjects who can express their own pleasure, their own desire."[11]

Materiality, as explained above, pays attention to "how the film is constructed" and how it "engages with bodies and with the matter of the world" (Olivieri 2012, p. 10). For Hongisto, the main way in which politically committed documentary films participate in "the real as process" (Hongisto 2015, p. 12) is through framing. Taking Hongisto's question as a starting point, we intend to answer the following questions: How do our two case studies (re)frame reality? How do they entangle diverse narrative waves through the editing?

Cuidado, resbala exposes the discrimination encountered by domestic workers within an economics framework that places care labour in the hidden part of the iceberg sustaining the markets. Following Bill Nichols's typology of modes of representation in documentary cinema (2010), we can describe it as an observational–participatory documentary film, with a couple of expository animated sequences, and a reflexive performative voice-over that opens and closes the film. We identify four different narrative waves: voices of domestic workers; interviews with academic experts; animation; and reflexive voice-over. Through a diffractive lens, we can visualise how these waves overlap within the

---

[8] A shorter version of the analysis of this film has been published in *Feminist Media Studies* (Calderón 2017).
[9] Replacing the term "disability" with that of "functional diversity" has been put forward in Spain by the "Movimiento Vida Independiente" (Independent Life Movement), which is articulated through a virtual community called "Foro de Vida Independiente" (Independent Life Forum), founded in 2001.
[10] The term cisgender, as opposed to transgender, refers to those people whose gender identity matches the sex that they were assigned at birth.
[11] "El postporno lo que intenta hacer es coger el lenguaje visual del porno corriente que tanto configura nuestra idea de lo que es la sexualidad, y darle la vuelta, politizarlo y aquéllos que eran objetos, convertirlos en sujetos que enuncian su propio placer, su propio deseo." Antonio Centeno. Q&A session. 5 November 2016 in Granada. All translations in this article are ours.

film editing, hence revealing that the diverse and apparently disconnected insights on care labour are actually entangled. This strategy allows us to place at the same level two narrative waves: the voices of the domestic workers and the voices of the academic experts interviewed for the film (Amaia Pérez Orozco, Yayo Herrero, and Mercedes Cordero). Knowledge is thus produced in a horizontal way, entangling insights from personal experience with those from academic backgrounds.

A third wave is visualised with the animated sequence in which a female voice-over explains the intersections of gender, class and nationality in the global care chain: women from the Global South that have migrated to the Global North are being exploited as domestic workers, so that women from the so-called first countries can conciliate their professions with household chores. Neither men, nor industries, nor the State assume any responsibility for care labour. Some care services are privatised, but as a whole, this only aggravates inequalities. The reflexive performative voice over belongs to Carolina Suárez Rasmussen, one of the film directors and a migrant from Argentina who worked as a domestic worker in Spain for three years.

The opening and closing sequences of the film with the reflexive voice over constitute a fourth narrative wave. The film starts with Suárez Rasmussen's testimony about finding out that domestic labour does not have the same legal status as other jobs, and finishes with her account of how the personal conflicts she has faced are connected with that fact, and thus have a collective political dimension. This testimony is key for reading *Cuidado, resbala* as a research journey, and what she is looking for is exactly what diffraction focuses on, i.e., "how different differences get made" (Barad 2007, p. 30). Throughout the film, the viewer is encouraged to recognise the way in which care labour is rendered invisible, labelled as different from other jobs within the patriarchal and neoliberal socio-economic system, placing the responsibility for life care on individuals, mainly women. These sequences also have the peculiarity of raising awareness of the camera, making it felt as embodied from a specific gaze. Such formal strategy subverts the conventional understanding of an objective gaze in documentary cinema. Moreover, the opening sequence asks the spectator to identify with the point of view of a female illegal immigrant who works as a domestic worker, a subject which de-centers masculinity and whiteness.

In *Yes, We Fuck!*, the representation of the rebellious and diverse bodies of the filmed subjects questions pathology, monstrosity, voyeuristic curiosity and/or pitiful solidarity. Instead, the filmed subjects are presented as both, desiring and desirable through the intra-actions which take place both sides of the camera. The film consists of six ten-minute stories which could be analysed, we propose, as different narrative waves which provide spectators with diverse entry points. We listen to the filmed subjects' discourses but we also observe their practices, engaging in various sexual activities that fall out of what Gayle Rubin calls the "charmed circle of sex" (Rubin [1984] 2006, p. 153).[12] Not only do their bodies deviate from ableist, racist and heterosexist norms but their sexualities also question androcentric, heteronormative and patriarchal conventions.

Yes, We Fuck! is a realist film whose main modes of representation are observational and participatory, though it also incorporates a performative mode in two of its stories. The first story works as a fist narrative wave in its setting the potential alliance between functional diversity and queer activists, stemming from the fact that their bodies do not fit within the productive norms. During a postporn workshop sequence, the observational-participatory mode of representation is combined with a poetic voice over which accompanies the images of group sex, in which sexualisation goes beyond the genitals and incorporates intra-actions between human and non-human artefacts. Centeno

---

[12] Rubin explains that, in western heteronormative societies, sex is regulated by a sexual value system. Within the charmed circle of so-called good and natural sexuality we find that which is "heterosexual, marital, monogamous, reproductive, and non-commercial." Moreover, "it should be coupled, relational, within the same generation, and occur at home. It should not involve pornography, fetish objects, sex toys of any sort, or roles other than male and female. Any sex that violates these rules is 'bad', 'abnormal', or 'unnatural'." (Rubin [1984] 2006, p. 152).

participates in the workshop, while the intra-actions between De La Morena and his camera with the rest of the bodies are expressed in very close shots, getting out of focus several times.

The second story presents a second wave by focusing on a heterosexual couple traversed by two visible differences: the functional diversity of Miriam, paraplegic, and the nationality of Pama, a migrant from India. The main mode of representation in this story is the observational-participatory one. In the interview with the couple, Pama hardly speaks and shows difficulty in communicating in Spanish. While she has an elaborated political discourse on sexuality and diversity, he uses very short phrases. What she emphasises is that due to his different cultural background, his gaze towards her is different, which she finds surprising. Since the story only lasts ten minutes, the characters' profiles and their relationship dynamics remain on a superficial level. The last scene, in which they have sexual intercourse, could be regarded as voyeuristic were it not for the fact that, within this story and in the film as a whole, the camera's voyeuristic gaze is constantly questioned (this is clear, for example, in stories four and six).

The third story also has an observational-participatory mode of representation. As a third narrative wave, it shows a BDSM session between a sex worker and a man with cerebral palsy. The fact that Linda is a female sex worker filmed by a man, wearing clothes associated with the figure of the dominatrix in mainstream porn, renders these sequences problematic, as they reproduce an objectifying and fetishistic gaze.[13] There's, however, a counterbalance that has to be taken into consideration. Linda is also presented with close-ups of her face as she expresses her reasons for being a sex worker. It's important to note that Linda is a migrant from the Global South, from a Latin American country. She states that the first reason why she is a sex worker is because of the money, and only later does she elaborate on her political position "advocating for the freedom of bodies, the freedom of pleasure and the freedom in doing as we please with our own bodies, without any moral or political mandate" (Min. 21:26). Thus, the film does not hide the fact that precarity in a sexist, racist and classist society is a decisive factor behind the exercise of sex work, but by rendering visible Linda's confident testimony, it also argues against the stigmatisation and victimisation of sex workers. Another aspect worth mentioning is the fact that before the BDSM session, the dialogue between the characters emphasises consent, vulnerability and respect.

The fourth story starts with a sequence in which the performative mode of representation propitiates identification with Mertxe, a blind woman who also appears in the first story. During the first three minutes, the screen is totally black as we listen to her talking to a friend about a squirting workshop. The screen goes black again at the end of the story, as we listen to female moans of pleasure. Thus, the formal strategies employed in this fourth narrative wave question the ocularcentrism of dominant cinema, giving an example of a haptic visuality[14] that triggers physical memories of touch, smell and taste. The contrast between the images of one character's vagina with a speculum and his subsequent assertion in an interview, identifying "with the male gender" (Min. 34:53), provides an eloquent example of the film as a diffraction apparatus. In reading one sequence through the other, this cutting-together-apart[15] strategy renders visible gender performativity, as we see the disconnection between the body and the gender enacted by the same person.

The fifth story consists mainly of talking heads. Therefore, its mode of representation is observational-participatory. The organisation of the sequence, which presents first the opinions of people with intellectual diversity (Down syndrome) and then the opinions of their parents, establishes a clear contrast between sexuality as pleasure on the one hand, and reproduction as responsibility,

---

[13] According to Laura Mulvey (Mulvey [1975] 1988, p. 58), fetishism fragments the female character into fetish images, such as her legs or her high-heel shoes.
[14] In haptic cinema, the scopophilic drive is replaced by the pleasure evoked by other senses, thus opening up a synaesthetic dimension.
[15] Agential cuts, according to Barad, do not produce absolute separations, but an agential situated separability, "a 'holding together' of the disparate itself" (Barad 2012, p. 46).

on the other. The story does not take sides, nor does it go deeper into problematic issues such as sterilisation, which is only superficially raised. What is emphasised in this fifth wave is the sexual desires of people with intellectual diversity together with the freedom and openness with which they talk about their own sexuality. In this sense, talking heads emerge as an empowering tool for people who express and affirm themselves in front of the camera.

The last story, sixth narrative wave, introduces the figure of the sexual assistant, which is different from the sex worker in the third story. The sexual assistant helps a person with functional diversity have access to her/his own body, without becoming herself/himself engaged in sexual intercourse. This story resorts to a performative mode of representation because the characters record themselves. Most of the sequence is shot from the sexual assistant's point of view (Teo) as he caresses the body of a quadriplegic woman. The beginning and the end of the sequence, where Teo removes and puts back on the lens cap, raises awareness of the camera, directly interpellating the audience before the credits start. The two characters look directly into the camera as they say why they are recording the video: "Visualising all of this is important. It is also important to help people with functional diversity discover it since we don't know that we can ask for it and that it is within our rights" (Min. 55:49). In each story, the characters make explicit their position as politically informed. In this case, the filmed subjects assert that making the film itself is their political/activist intervention.

None of the film characters fit within the androcentric norm, let alone within the mainstream pornography standards of desirable bodies. Female pleasure and gender performativity are also key issues: there are transgender characters in three out of the six stories, and female characters embrace and openly discuss their sexual pleasure. In general, gender is considered as oppressive, but also as something that can be questioned and subverted. Indeed, *Yes, We Fuck!* has become a tool for alliances between Spanish activist groups, which have been called "Alianzas Tullido-Transfeministas", i.e., Crip-Queer Alliances (García-Santesmases Fernández et al. 2017).[16]

Our second tool, performativity, is connected with this understanding of the production process of the films as a political action in itself and their becoming militant objects. In the previous section we described documentary as a performative act that captures some sort of reality in-the-making that results from the intervention of the camera and/or the film production. And paraphrasing Butler, we proposed performativity as a way of naming the power of documentary cinema, conceived not as representation but as apparatus, "to bring about a new situation or to set into motion a set of effects" (Butler 2015, p. 28).

Cuidado, resbala was conceived as political from the beginning, not only in terms of content, but also in its production process. For Leonor Jiménez, the only professional filmmaker out of the six directors, the assembly-like method they carried out was very different from what she had been taught at film school:

Because normally, within the world of documentary and audiovisual creation, a lot of emphasis is placed on the author's gaze, which is individual and hierarchical. That person has to have a gaze of their own. And we were proposing exactly the opposite. (Jiménez et al. 2017)[17]

Jiménez emphasises that their being a group of feminist women was indeed a difference that mattered and had effects on their way of working, especially in terms of power relations. The creation of an empathetic and trusting atmosphere was also a fundamental aspect during the recording of the interviews. Clear explanations about who they were, what the film was about and why they had

---

[16] Transfeminism keeps on working with the political subject "women", but advocates for a subject of feminism that includes other subjectivities, in as much as gender and the biological differences employed in the legitimisation of social inequalities do not only oppress women but also all those who do not fit within androcentric norms, such as queer individuals and people with functional diversity.

[17] "Porque normalmente desde el mundo así de la creación documental, audiovisual, hacen mucho hincapié en la mirada del autor o de la autora. Una mirada individual, el autor, jerárquica; esa persona tiene que tener una mirada propia. Y nosotras estábamos planteando todo lo contrario." Leonor Jiménez. Personal interview. 23 January 2017 in Málaga.

contacted the person for an interview contributed to reduce, albeit a little, "the issue of the camera as an invasive power element"[18]. They remember that a turning point in the making of *Cuidado, resbala* took place after the distressing interview with two domestic workers from Nicaragua. That's when they decided they had to look for alternatives so as to move from the personal to the collective and to avoid focusing only on victimisation. With the women from "Territorio Doméstico" they saw these possibilities materialised.

The importance that the film gives to global care chains and to the experience of women immigrants was not something deliberately present in their agenda, but an issue that arose as undeniable evidence. As Carolina Suárez summarises it: "If we talk about vulnerabilities or unequal treatment, I think that here all three things come together: being a woman, a migrant, and a domestic worker."[19] According to her, *Cuidado, resbala* is a feminist documentary because it "questions, criticises and highlights all the contradictions of the patriarchal system and its economic correlate, which is capitalism" (Jiménez et al. 2017) Jiménez reckons that the film can actually be called radically feminist, in the sense that it goes to the roots of placing care at the centre of the system.

The film official premiere was at the 16th edition of the Málaga Film Festival in 2013. Produced with public funds, it did not have any commercial distribution and they stopped sending it to festivals when they realised that it was being asked for by lots of associations, workshops and seminars, which, from their point of view, were the main exhibition spaces. That's why they decided to put it online for free.[21] In a similar way to that in which second wave feminists employed documentary films as a militant tool, some of the domestic workers who appear in *Cuidado, resbala* have used it in diverse forums to raise awareness and empower people who experience similar situations. For instance, "Territorio Doméstico" has organised projections at the "Eskalera Karakola" feminist space in Madrid, with the purpose of rendering visible their demands.

In the case of *Yes, We Fuck!*, Centeno admits that it was thanks to the contribution of researcher and anthropologist Andrea García-Santesmases that he and De la Morena found out that there were people already working with diverse sexual representations in feminist postporn cinema. They had not thought about the gender axis when they started working on the project but as they moved forward, it became one of their main insights:

> *What has subsequently been the central and most powerful axis of the documentary is that the gender axis and the axis of functional diversity are the same axes practically. I mean, in the end, the structure of oppression is the same, isn't it? That attempt to justify social inequalities because of biological differences is a very old story and that is why the discourses are so parallel and so related.* (Centeno 2016)[22]

The production process of the film, and later on, its exhibition have been spaces for the encounter of these activisms. Looking at *Yes, We Fuck!* as a diffraction apparatus, rather than as a reflecting mirror that reproduces the same elsewhere, we can argue that the various narrative waves through which the axes of gender, sexuality and functional diversity are co-constructed by Centeno and De La Morena produce, facilitate and solicit new ways of seeing the intersections and alliances between these three axes (Minh-ha 2005, p. 13).

---

[18] "Eso de la cámara como elemento invasivo y de poder" Leonor Jiménez. Personal interview. 23 January 2017 in Málaga.
[19] "Si hablamos de vulnerabilidades o de desigual trato, yo creo que ahí se juntan las tres cosas. Por ser mujer, por ser migrante, por ser empleada doméstica." Carolina Suárez. Personal interview. 23 January 2017 in Málaga.
[21] Vimeo website. Date of access: 20 February 2019. https://vimeo.com/67552738.
[22] "Lo que luego ha sido el eje central y potente del documental que es que, el eje de género y el eje de diversidad funcional son el mismo eje prácticamente, o sea, que al final la estructura de opresión es la misma, ¿no? Ese intento de, de intentar justificar las desigualdades sociales a partir de las diferencias biológicas es una historia muy vieja y que por eso los discursos son tan paralelos y tan afines." Antonio Centeno. Skype interview. 20 November 2016.

It's important to mention that in the Spanish context, there's a strong feminist debate about the abolition of prostitution or its legalisation as sex work.[23] Centeno is in favour of the latter and has defended sexual assistance as a right for people with functional diversity within the Spanish Independent Life Movement. In this regard he states that: "Those in favour of the abolition of prostitution can incorporate the reality of functional diversity into the process of constructing a general human sexuality that is rich and appreciative of difference, so as to eliminate the demand for sexual services beyond police repression" (Centeno Ortiz 2014, p. 109).[24]

We finally come to our last tool, i.e., emotionality. How does making/watching these films affect subjects and objects on both sides of the camera and the screen? How do emotions produce the surfaces and boundaries that delineate the individual and the social? (Ahmed 2014, p. 10).

As mentioned before, several testimonies in *Cuidado, resbala* evoke anger and distress. The opening and closing sequences, with the reflexive voice over and the embodied subjective camera, perform entrapment and despair. These feelings are strong when domestic workers find themselves isolated. The turning point comes with the movement from individual struggle towards organised collective action with the testimonies of the women from "Territorio Doméstico", the interviews with academic experts who envision alternatives, and the festive demonstrations. The main emotions evoked in the film and gathered by the audiences have to do with empowerment, hope, pride and solidarity.

Similarly, the film subjects and spectators of *Yes, We Fuck!* have praised the sex-positive tone of the film. Even though several testimonies evoke shame, anger and discomfort, the film performs mainly positive emotions such as pleasure, love, trust, freedom and curiosity. As in the case of *Cuidado, resbala*, positive emotions become stronger when the struggle becomes open and collective. For instance, Soledad Arnau, the main character of the story about sexual assistance and a feminist functional diversity activist, describes her experience in the film as very positive:

All the stories have enriched me a great deal, and of course mine, well, I would not change the experience I had for anything, what I felt in that screening. Because for me it was like a before and after. I think it's a beautiful way to learn to love oneself, to love oneself even more, if I already loved myself then even more, and also to love the body because in the end, I think it's impossible to love yourself if you do not love your body (. . . .) To have a body is not something problematic, I believe it is the most beautiful thing in the world to have a body and to be able to enjoy it. And fortunately the documentary is an example, it shows that bodies are enjoyable. (Arnau 2018)[25]

To conservative, paternalistic, heteronormative and ableist material-discursive practices, the filmmakers and filmed subjects of *Yes, We Fuck!* respond with their performative right to appear as desiring and desirable subjects.

5. Three Effects of Feminist Material-Discursive Practices in Documentary Cinema

In this final section, we diffractively read insights raised by each of our case studies to illustrate three effects that feminist material-discursive practices in documentary cinema can have. The first effect is that both films operate as feminist countervisuality devices that reframe realities from a gender

---

[23] Instances of this are the steps towards the abolition of prostitution taken recently by the Spanish socialist government and their contestation from sex workers associations, attempting to create a sex workers trade union.

[24] "Quien esté por la abolición de la prostitución, puede incorporar la realidad de la diversidad funcional al proceso de construir una sexualidad humana general suficientemente rica y positivamente apreciadora de la diferencia como para eliminar la demanda de servicios sexuales más allá de la represión policial."

[25] "Todas las historias me enriquecen muchísimo y desde luego la mía, bueno, no cambiaría por nada del mundo la vivencia que viví, que sentí en esa proyección. Porque para mí fue como un antes y un después. Yo creo que es una forma preciosa de aprender a quererse a una misma, a quererse más todavía, si ya me quería pues ahora más todavía, y bueno también a querer al cuerpo porque al final, creo que es imposible quererte si no te quieres el cuerpo (…) realmente no es nada problemático, es lo más hermoso del mundo tener un cuerpo, creo yo y poder disfrutar de este cuerpo. Y afortunadamente el documental es un ejemplo de que los cuerpos son disfrutables." Soledad Arnau. Q&A Session. 16 October 2018 at the University of Granada.

aware perspective. A pattern that both films share is that the filmed subjects are empowered as they enact their right to appear as political subjects in the public space.

In *Yes, We Fuck!*, rebellious and diverse bodies are presented in a way that questions their intelligibility from the perspectives of pathology and/or pitiful paternalism. In their sexually explicit images, the filmed subjects enact their performative right to appear as both, desiring and desirable. In *Cuidado, resbala*, care labour is placed at the centre of the economic activities. The filmmakers render visible inequalities connected with three factors: being a woman, a migrant, and a domestic worker. But they also propose real alternatives, showing the organised collective struggles of domestic workers and reading these insights from personal activist experience through those from feminist academic experts.

The second effect of feminist material-discursive practices in these films is their rendering visible the ways in which patterns of difference are turned into and/or employed by structures of inequality. In *Cuidado, resbala*, this is approached within the framework of the sexual division of labour. In the animated sequence, a female voice-over explains the intersections of gender, class and nationality in the transnational care chain. In the case of *Yes, We Fuck!*, Centeno admitted that directing this film made him realise that the feminist struggle and the struggle of people with functional diversity have various aspects in common: from their political work with the body, to the critical dismantling of the attempt to justify social inequalities arguing biological differences.

The third effect of feminist material-discursive practices that we diffractively read in these films has to do with the move from "reflecting on representations" to "accounting for how practices matter" (Barad 2007, p. 90). The directors of *Cuidado, resbala* and *Yes, We Fuck!* envisioned the production process of both films as a political action in itself. In *Cuidado, resbala*, the directors render visible inequalities faced by domestic workers, but they also visualise other possibilities for liveable conditions. The film evokes anger and distress with various testimonies, but rather than victimisation and paralysis, awareness of injustice is portrayed as leading to collective struggles. The subjects in *Yes, We Fuck!* accepted to appear in the film because they shared an understanding of the need to create a different collective imaginary. Through the co-organisation of filmed workshops, the production process operated as a space for the encounter of queer and crip activisms that had been mostly disconnected until then and that have continued working together since.

If we recognise the onto-epistemological potential of documentaries to "co-compose the real" (Hongisto 2015, p. 12), we can envision their ethico-political impact in the opening up of possibilities for gender and world making otherwise. The processes of making and watching feminist documentary films can co-create spaces for breaking the silence about precarious situations and for collectively generating more livable conditions. The two films that we have referred to manage to find a paradoxical balance pointed out by Butler: The filmed subjects—domestic workers, people with functional diversity, transgender activists—are presented as "at once vulnerable and capable of resistance" (Butler 2015, p. 141). Films like *Cuidado, resbala* and *Yes, We Fuck!* exemplify the capability of looking back and beyond androcentric visuality regimes.

Author Contributions: Article conceptualization, O.C.-S. and A.S.-E.; interviews, O.C.-S.; methodology and primary analysis, O.C.-S. and A.S.-E.; original draft preparation, O.C.-S.; review and editing, O.C.-S. and A.S.-E.; supervision, A.S.-E.; project administration, project design and funding acquisition A.S.-E.

Funding: This work is part of GRACE Gender and Cultures of Equality in Europe, a European Union's Horizon 2020 research and innovation programme under the Marie Skłodowska-Curie grant agreement No. 675378. The research has been funded by this project. The GRACE Project is led by Suzanne Clisby at the University of Hull. Adelina Sánchez-Espinosa is Principal Investigator at the University of Granada.

Conflicts of Interest: The authors declare no conflict of interest. The funders had no role in the design of the study; in the collection, analyses, or interpretation of data; in the writing of the manuscript, or in the decision to publish the results.

References

Ahmed, Sara. 2014. *The Cultural Politics of Emotion*, 2nd ed. Edinburgh: Edinburgh University Press.
Arnau, Soledad. 2018. Q&A Session at the University of Granada. October 16.
Barad, Karen. 2007. *Meeting the Universe Halfway: Quantum Physics and the Entanglement of Matter and Meaning*. Durham and London: Duke University Press.
Barad, Karen. 2012. Nature's Queer Performativity. *Kvinder, Køn og forskning/Women, Gender and Research* 1: 25–53. [CrossRef]
Belia, Vasiliki. 2015. You can read your way out of this. A diffractive reading of Alison Bechdel's Are You My Mother? with Virginia Woolf and Adrienne Rich. Master's thesis, Universiteit Utrecht, Utrecht, The Netherlands. Available online: https://dspace.library.uu.nl/handle/1874/320655 (accessed on 18 April 2019).
Bruzzi, Stella. 2000. *New Documentary: A Critical Introduction*. London and New York: Routledge.
Butler, Judith. 1990. *Gender Trouble: Feminism and the Subversion of Identity*. New York and London: Routledge.
Butler, Judith. 2015. *Notes Toward a Performative Theory of Assembly*. Cambridge, Massachusetts and London: Harvard University Press.
Calderón, Orianna. 2017. Feminist documentary cinema as a diffraction apparatus for the visualisation of care labour: the Spanish collective film Cuidado, resbala (2013). *Feminist Media Studies* 17: 308–12. [CrossRef]
Cano Abadía, Mónica. 2017. Agencia crítica y desposesión. La actualidad de la pregunta por la libertad en Judith Butler. *ISEGORÍA Revista de filosofía moral y política* 56: 263–77. [CrossRef]
Centeno, Antonio. 2016. Skype interview. November 20.
Centeno Ortiz, Antonio. 2014. Simbolismos y alianzas para una revuelta de los cuerpos. *Educació Social Revista d'Intervenció Socioeducativa* 58: 101–18. Available online: https://www.raco.cat/index.php/EducacioSocial/article/view/284939/372790 (accessed on 18 April 2019).
Cuidado, resbala. 2013. Directed by María Camacho Gómez, Montserrat Clos Fabuel, Mercedes Cordero Suárez, Vanessa Gómez Martínez, Carolina Suárez Rasmussen and Leonor Jiménez Moreno. Málaga: La Mirada Invertida and Círculo de Mujeres. Available online: https://vimeo.com/67552738 (accessed on 20 February 2019).
García-Santesmases Fernández, Andrea, Nuria Vergés Bosch, and Elisabet Almeda Samaranch. 2017. "From Alliance to Trust": Constructing Crip-Queer Intimacies. *Journal of Gender Studies* 26: 1–13. [CrossRef]
Haraway, Donna. 2004. The Promises of Monsters: A Regenerative Politics for Inappropriate/d Others. In *The Haraway Reader*. New York and London: Routledge, pp. 63–124. First published 1992.
Haraway, Donna. 2000. *How Like a Leaf. An Interview with Thyrza Nichols Godeve*. New York and Oxon: Routledge.
Hongisto, Ilona. 2015. *Soul of the Documentary. Framing, Expression, Ethics*. Amsterdam: Amsterdam University Press. [CrossRef]
Jiménez, Leonor, Carolina Suárez, and Montserrat Clos. 2017. Personal interview. Málaga, January 23.
Johnston, Claire. 2000. Women's Cinema as Counter-cinema. In *Feminism and Film*. Edited by E. Ann Kaplan. Oxford: Oxford University Press, pp. 22–33. First published 1973.
Kaiser, Birgit Mara. 2014. Worlding CompLit: Diffractive Reading with Barad, Glissant and Nancy. *Parallax* 20: 274–87. [CrossRef]
Kuhn, Annette. 1994. *Women's Pictures. Feminism and Cinema*, 2nd ed. London: Verso.
Lesage, Julia. 1984. Feminist Documentary: Aesthetics and Politics. In *Show us Life. Toward a History and Aesthetics of the Committed Documentary*. Edited by Thomas Waugh. London: The Scarecrow Press, pp. 223–51.
Lukic, Jasmina, and Adelina Sánchez-Espinosa. 2011. Feminist Approaches to Close Reading. In *Theories and Methodologies in Postgraduate Feminist Research. Researching Differently*. Edited by Rosemarie Buikema, Gabrielle Griffin and Nina Lykke. London: Routledge, pp. 85–160.
Miller-Young, Mireille, Tristan Taormino, Celine Parreñas Shimizu, and Constance Penley. 2013. Introduction: The Politics of Producing Pleasure. In *The Feminist Porn Book. The Politics of Producing Pleasure*. Edited by Miller-Young Mireille, Tristan Taormino, Celine Parreñas Shimizu and Constance Penley. New York: The Feminist Press at the City University of New York, pp. 9–20.
Minh-ha, Trinh T. 2005. *The Digital Film Event*. New York: Routledge.
Mirzoeff, Nicholas. 2011. The Right to Look. *Critical Inquiry* 37: 473–96. [CrossRef]
Mulvey, Laura. 1988. Visual Pleasure and Narrative Cinema. In *Feminism and Film Theory*. Edited by Constance Penley. New York and London: Routledge, pp. 57–68. First published 1975.

Nichols, Bill. 2010. *Introduction to Documentary*, 2nd ed. Bloomington: Indiana University Press.
Olivieri, Domitilla. 2012. Haunted by Reality. Toward a Feminist Study of Documentary Film: Indexicality, Vision and the Artifice. Ph.D. thesis, Universiteit Utrecht, Utrecht, The Netherlands. Available online: https://dspace.library.uu.nl/handle/1874/221965 (accessed on 18 April 2019).
Revelles Benavente, Beatriz. 2014. Literature, Gender and Communication in the Making: Understanding Toni Morrison's Work in the Information Society. Ph.D. thesis, Universitat Oberta de Catalunya, Barcelona, Spain. Available online: https://www.tdx.cat/handle/10803/306597?locale-attribute=en (accessed on 18 April 2019).
Rubin, Gayle. 2006. Thinking Sex: Notes for a Radical Theory of the Politics of Sexuality. In *Culture, Society and Sexuality*. Edited by Aggleton Peter and Richard Parker. New York and London: Routledge, pp. 143–78. First published 1984.
Rubira García, Rainer, Puebla Martínez Belén, and Gelado Marcos Roberto. 2018. Social Representations in Studying Information, Knowledge, and Mediations: A Critical Review. *Social Sciences* 7: 256. [CrossRef]
Union Maids. 1976. Directed by Jim Klein, Miles Mogulescu and Julia Reichert. Ohio: New Day Films.
Wollen, Peter. 2002. Godard and Counter-Cinema. Vent d'Est. In *The European Cinema Reader*. Edited by Catherine Fowler. London and New York: Routledge, pp. 74–82. First published 1972.
Yes, We Fuck!. 2015. Directed by Antonio Centeno and Raúl de la Morena. Barcelona: Centeno, De la Morena and crowdfunding. Available online: https://vimeo.com/123177395 (accessed on 20 February 2019).

 © 2019 by the authors. Licensee MDPI, Basel, Switzerland. This article is an open access article distributed under the terms and conditions of the Creative Commons Attribution (CC BY) license (http://creativecommons.org/licenses/by/4.0/).

Article

The Sonic Intra-Face of a Noisy Feminist Social Kitchen

Juliana España Keller

Victorian College of the Arts, University of Melbourne, Melbourne, VIC 3006, Australia; info@julianaespanakeller.com

Received: 7 May 2019; Accepted: 19 August 2019; Published: 23 August 2019

Abstract: This paper asks what is the value of transforming the kitchen into a sonic performative work and public site for art and social practice. A Public Kitchen is formed by recreating the private and domestic space of a kitchen into a public space through a sonic performance artwork. The kitchen table is a platform for exploring, repositioning and amplifying kitchen tools as material phenomena through electronic and manual manipulation into an immersive sonic performance installation. This platform becomes a collaborative social space, where somatic movement and sensory, sonic power of the repositioned kitchen tools are built on a relational architecture of iterative sound performances that position the art historical and the sociopolitical, transforming disciplinary interpretations of the body and technology as something that is not specifically exclusively human but post-human. A Public Kitchen represents a pedagogical strategy for organizing and responding collectively to the local, operating as an independent nomadic event that speaks through a creative practice that is an unfolding process. (Re)imagining the social in a Public Kitchen produces noisy affects in a sonic intra-face that can contribute to transforming our social imaginations, forming daring dissonant narratives that feed post-human ethical practices and feminist genealogies. This paper reveals what matters—a feminist struggle invaluable in channeling the intra-personal; through the entanglement of the self, where language, meaning and subjectivity are relational to human difference and to what is felt from the social, what informs from a multi-cultural nomadic existence and diffractive perspective. The labored body is entangled with post-human contingencies of food preparation, family and social history, ritual, tradition, social geography, local politics, and women's oppression; and is resonant and communicates as a site where new sonic techniques of existence are created and experiences shared.

Keywords: sound and noise art; feminist new materialism; posthumanities; doing-cooking; social engagement; participatory practices

---

Preface

This paper needs to expand out from the page for the reader. Firstly, and most obviously, it offers a written analysis of the artwork and emphasizes the relation to Martha Rosler's seminal work, *Semiotics of the Kitchen* (Rosler 1975). A Public Kitchen responds to the historical, socio-political, feminist academic research in relation to the Special Issue on Feminist New Materialisms. Secondly, visual images of various performance iterations provide useful illustration. Finally, this text offers a link to the sound performance work, 'The Kitchen Shift' that can be accessed online. This audio-visual documentation can be found on my website with the following hyperlink listed below. By using this link, the reader is connected to the art work directly. This adjunct helps elucidate a fuller understanding of a Public Kitchen.

This journal paper forms part of the artwork and research, *A Public Kitchen*, which is foremost a collective performance work and immersive sound installation. When reading this text, there is a desire and need (by the artist) for the reader to experience the collective sensory and sonic attributes of a Public Kitchen; however, the live and immersive experience of performance art, or live art, is at once irreplaceable or not easily substituted. The artwork is thus always to be set-up each time for an indeterminate and distinct outcome with room for failure and noisy slippages. A Public Kitchen is a culturally constructed representation of reality and positions what is possible and what it is not possible in its activation. As there have been many iterations of this work to date—spanning geographies and social groups (2015–2019)—much vital material has been generated over time in the form of audio-visual documentation.[1]

1. Introduction

> "dare take the risk of affirmative politics and the collective construction of social horizons of hope" (Rosi Braidotti 2014).

The research generated by the artwork, a Public Kitchen, contributes to feminist new materialist discourse by making the notion of human–non-human agency graspable as a creative act that cuts across pre-established dichotomies, by transversing hierarchies of power relations that organize human life as contextualized in by new materialist theorists Barad and Braidotti (Barad 2003, 2007; Braidotti 2002, 2013). Through the medium of sound, I am investigating; emphasizing entities, ethics, social class, and social political intervention in the process. This subjectivity illuminates and activates how we move through the world, react to surroundings and respond to everything. It also shows how the normative and hierarchical relations amongst human groups based on race, sexuality, social class, and ability are always intimately entangled with the broader political economies/ecologies of which we are a part. The performance artwork establishes a scaffold for thinking about a range of ideas of what is felt through encounters with philosophy, sonic arts, community participation, feminist materialism, and post-human thought.

The human and non-human relation to machines and machine learning is enacted through intra-active entanglement; since it represents an active pedagogy practice for organizing, facilitating and responding collectively to the local activated as Andrew Murphie states on how to anarchive[2] through: "the ability to find a way out of systems, often from within to life's living"(Murphie 2016, p. 5). A noisy kitchen is felt as a musical sounding in the everyday rhythm of lived intensities and is seen as Brian Massumi (2002) posits *"a repertory of traces* of collaborative research-creation events" and "platforms for organizing and orienting live, collaborative *encounters"* (Murphie 2016, p. 6). Agency is conjured through the doing-cooking[3] of the kitchen to create a sonic recipe[4] as the becoming of the human–non-human relationship to uncover the paradigms that shape-shift performance art.

This paper focuses on the unpacking of a creative practice, resonating with agency and amplifying where the experiential is intensely experienced as "creating together", foregrounding a way to move forward pedagogically and experientially (Conrad and Sinner 2015; Manning 2016). A Public Kitchen is embedded in the social, and the artwork allows for human slippages, failures that form part of the work. In particular, it considers how feminist new materialism can create daring dissonant narratives that feed post-human ethical practices and feminist genealogies. This research reveals what matters—a feminist struggle invaluable in highlighting and responding collectively to the local with a systemic understanding of material phenomena in an immersive sonic performative installation. This

---

[1] The creative artwork and exhibition titled: "The Kitchen Shift" can be found here: https://vimeo.com/332604174. The Password: THEKITCHENSHIFT OR on the artist's website: http://cargocollective.com/julianaespanakeller/THE-KITCHEN-SHIFT-THE-INDUSTRIAL-SCHOOL-BUILDING.

[2] The word 'anarchive' comes from the "The Go-To How to Book of Anarchiving" by Andrew Murphie of the Senselab (Murphie 2016).

[3] The entanglement of "doing-cooking"—a term coined by Michel de Certeau (de Certeau et al. 2014).

[4] A *sonic recipe* is a dynamic arrangement of sound/noise material generated through the artwork by the intersection of the human–non-human, embracing the critical potentiality of a vital matter in a sonic apparatus.

position seeks to ignite and transform our social imagination and deactivate pervasive and dominating patriarchal ethico-politics.

Finally, this paper explores ways in which post-humanist and new materialist thinking can be put to work in order to (re)imagine a more open perspective in approaching and pursuing community-based, collaborative practices underscored pedagogically and rhizomatically as a teaching about gender and a politics of care (Revelles-Benavente and Ramos 2017; Kumar 2002). What performance practices can do is contribute, co-produce through a constellation of variables of agency and become activated in a collaborative learning experience (Strom and Martin 2017). It is an invitation to scholars of posthumanism and new materialism to imagine how creative ideas and processual thinking might be put to work through performative practices with fluidity, flux, expansion and understanding of difference. In observation, anarchiving pertains to the event and live art that is activated through a performative cross-platform phenomenon where humanity is something that needs more humanizing as we move forward to challenging times ahead, where participation is risky and where research-creation can be contextualized performatively as co-constructed. In this way, human–non-humans, actions, or events are defined by their relations and function as part of an assemblage[5] that is concerned with processual work and self-transformation. (Huybrechts 2014; Torrens 2014). What is correlative to intra-corporeality—where the artwork is an aesthetic, psychological and physical experience—is how these entanglements mesh with our perceptions; where the mediation of affect as a sound performance plays out and functions as a reading of the bodies of others.

2. Starting from the Middle

Eight individuals in identical dresses file robotically in through a portal door. They walk, one after the next, into a space that is embedded with history, bringing their ways of moving materiality into the present. Heavy, heavier, heaviest. They walk in formation, masks on, heads high, hands up, carried above their chest, ready to work in thick, yellow, rubber utilitarian gloves. Each individual picks a spot in the room and stares out at the audience with a dead-pan face. One of the members picks up her guitar and begins to play doom-drone riffs. The sound does not rock, as much as crush[6] inexorably, until the rest of the group move out collectively into the performative space with their bodies and making their way over to the kitchen table—the motherboard—to join her. Their self/bodies move through the space, shifting into various somatic positions on the floor, against the wall, with each other. The figure/ground choreographic relation between the human and this historical place dissolves as the outline of the human is traversed by substantial material intra-changes; the prelude of oneself as transcendent, generated through and entangled with other systems, processes and events. Their shiny bodies cannot resist the allure of shiny objects waiting on the motherboard, considering the effects they have, from manufacture to disposability, while reckoning with the strange agencies that intra-connect substance, flesh and place on a deep molecular level. Vibrating, vibrating . . . the sound distils and subtracts, and then the vocals begin resonating, looping in and generating live outbursts from the artist who is writing these words now, plunging the sound into a human-non-human realm of culinary noise abstraction. Rubber gloves smack back at you. The sonic recipe is in effect.

Here, I begin by writing to you from the middle of a Public Kitchen, as the words are moving across and through the whole final creative artwork. The middle is for me a happening of writing and research that emerges from my own personal experience combined with an art practice that requires a sensitivity, or attunement, to what moves through thought and thinking as a performance artist—a

---

[5] "Assemblage" is a material affective dynamic in which bodies become "other" to themselves (Deleuze et al. 1987). However, my understanding moves further in the direction of post-humanist feminist epistemology and quantum physics, as outlined in the works of Donna Haraway and Karen Barad. In turn, difference is relational to the concept of "becoming" explained by Barad and Braidotti. In this paper, I am articulating that participating with other bodies in a Public Kitchen is thus a learning process and can be used as a pedagogical tool to understand others.

[6] The word "crush" describes noise as "coming on," or putting sonic pressure on something.

maker of live art.[7] I am creating a relation to the person who is reading this paper, by moving into a thinking process that (re)constructs our interdependence with the human and nonhuman, beginning with thinking and acting diffractively[8] and intra-actively[9] without discrediting the consideration for collectivity and *the other*[10] and all the challenges of foregrounding this artwork. A Public Kitchen creates an opening, unfolding as a performative choreography; it is a creative event that communicates, acts and behaves in a social space, all the way down to the molecular level, not too rigidly conformist, but a writing canvas for the one, or the few, who speak to many. She rises.

A *Public Kitchen* is defined as a sonic performance with innumerable potential iterations as a technique for making research-creation across geographical locations, made possible via an immersive sculptural apparatus and active human participation. The participants in this social artwork are women, or those who identify as women, inclusive of gender fluidity. In turn, the objects generate a sonic performance work that dramatizes the material agencies, flows and intensities between kitchen objects and humans. This is done by creating sonic recipes in a Public Kitchen installation space. Living always comes to terms with forms of dissonance emerging from a complex set of social conditions, such as the auditory experience of sound that lacks musical quality; the sound that is a disagreeable auditory experience as a form of noise. Sound matter is therefore generated by making these conditions/forces a constant process of engagement, where thinking and acting move 'from the middle out'—drawing on what is intrinsic or embedded, creating ways of shifting into each other and attuning to these fields of difference. A Public Kitchen can, therefore, be seen to represent an active pedagogy for organizing and responding collectively to the local, through a spectrum of sound phenomena where home is a middling, while still operating as an independent nomadic event with many, and potentially on-going, transnational iterations.

I argue that human–non-human intra-actions within sonic recipes are made apparent due to the doing of the action by the subject, paraphrasing Barad, being the context of the work; this makes the effects of the action relational in the real world (Barad 2003). Intra-action should not be confused with interaction, where elements exist first and then interact. Instead, an intra-action conceptualizes that it is the action between (and not in-between) that which matters; it is in the action that the elements themselves are produced interdependently. In turn, a sonic recipe (in which intra-actions can occur) is defined as a relational partition of electronic sound patterns that form a dynamic arrangement of sound/noise material composed with kitchen tools and appliances in a sonic performance installation (a Public Kitchen). Overall, sound phenomena materialize when the human and non-human are fully present and exercise a guiding or piloting role, affecting and working through what is organically presented in a particular iteration of a Public Kitchen event. Here, the idea of the participatory is critical, where the human and non-human fuse to take on a positive and affirmative character, aligning with Braidotti's understanding of an ethical practice, which is an ethico-politic stated in the opening quote of the introduction. I would also posit it as, what Braidotti distinguishes, "a break with the doxa": the acquiescent application of established norms and values by de-territorialising them and introducing an alternative ethic flows (Braidotti and Hlavajova 2018, p. 224).

I contend that a participatory sonic performance work precipitates a kitchen interior intra-subjectivity—a process evoking the specific entanglement of *doing-cooking* with *affect* by providing a complex assemblage of embedded and embodied thought, where the psyche and the body work in

---

[7] This thinking has been influenced immensely by Erin Manning, who conceptualizes "middling" as a way of thinking through the way the minor (a minor gesture that moves across the work) calls us to attend to something and moves us through thresholds of socialities and techniques in philosophy, art and activism (Manning 2019).

[8] (Barad 2007).

[9] (Barad 2003).

[10] In this journal paper, I am articulating that participating with other bodies in a Public Kitchen is thus a learning process and can be used as a pedagogical tool to understand others. I refer here to American philosopher and feminist scholar, Bell Hooks, and the intersectionality of race, capitalism, and gender, and what she describes as the ability to counter-act systems of women's oppression and class domination (Hooks 2000).

unison. What is correlative to intra-corporeality—where the artwork is an aesthetic, psychological and physical experience—is how these entanglements mesh with our perceptions; where the mediation of affect as a sound performance plays out and functions as a reading of the bodies of others. Within each iteration, each participant is triggered by the vibrational sensation of sound that rises to the surface through the mind/body. Affect can be felt as sound that behaves as active matter—to listen and absorb sound material activated through the playing of kitchen objects, deeply. This triggers physical movement felt in the transmission within and between bodies and objects.

3. Resonance in a Public Kitchen

Resonance in a Public kitchen addresses a deeply intertwined collective moment when the human and non-human intra-act in the apparatus of a Public Kitchen. To be clear, resonance is one of the fundamental phenomena, not just of acoustics or science in general. Resonance is a factor entangled with intra-activity and diffraction in the sonic intra-face of a Public Kitchen. The "resonance" experienced becomes a vital and transformative moment in the process, instigated by a "material turn". A critical live awareness occurs where sound (technological or non-technological) can be felt and seen collectively and affectively as an automated society coping with the demands of life with everyday technology. Thus, resonance in performance can be seen as a bridge to the post-human: to be attentive to the mutual accommodation or responsiveness of human and non-human agents. It is not mitigated from the outside to the inside of the body; it is already in the body and in the mind through active resonant forces. In turn, my position always returns to the sound that is produced in intra-activity. Within each iteration, each participant is triggered by the vibrational sensation of sound that rises to the surface through the mind/body with the gestural use of a contac mic that touches each kitchen tool as it is played. Affect can be felt as *sound that behaves as active matter*—to listen and absorb sound material activated through the playing of kitchen objects, deeply. This triggers physical movement felt in the transmission within and between bodies.

In turn, this research seeks to address resonant frequency characterized in the oscillation of sound, which can be observed as vibrational bodies performing with the kitchen objects (reverberating as an extension of the self). I argue that it must always be understood relationally, as vibration that is already materializing between humans and non-humans in intra-action. This also raises an awareness of the complexities involved with diffractive paradoxes of difference revealed in sonic relations and my own affective politics. In turn, sound works its way to the forefront of contemporary sensory behaviour in user experience, by sculpting, shifting and changing our perception of the kitchen environment in which the body labors to listen creatively. I argue that a Public Kitchen becomes an echo chamber of kitchen intensities that resonate amongst others, pushing thought toward its material forces of intra-actions to describe as Manning states, "pure experience in the in-folding of potential that keeps actual experience open to its more than" (Manning 2016, p. 29).

As Elaine Swan considers, there are colonial and anti-colonial dynamics at play between masculinity and femininity, specific ethnicities, multiculturalism, and imperialism, as I have explained in my footnote on "the other". I argue that these are evident in a Public Kitchen assemblage. I would also argue that these dynamics are seen as post-human indicators from which we can interrogate, more closely, the connection (imagined or not) between food and the Other. As a multicultural pedagogy that can perform and engender, this research and artwork certainly experiments with various encounters with 'otherness'; this is approached via a dialogical response to feminism, social class and domestic labor. In post-human terms, food has, as Swan states, "become a battleground for politics, policy, and reform" on many levels (Flowers and Swan 2011, p. 235).

In the context of transnational mobility, Ilaria Vanni attributes the sense of "being at home," or belonging to somewhere, as dissociated from a geographical location and replaced by belonging through specific everyday practices (Lloyd and Vasta 2017). This moving or roving idea is conceptualized in the Artists' Soup Kitchen, based in Toronto, Canada, where different artists host a lunch each week and bring their creative practices to a community table. Vanni makes us aware that the concept of home has been an intellectual obsession for a long time; where others try to pin down its meaning—and continue to revel in its multiplicity through the interactional achievement of people, spaces and things—the ambivalent nature of home-making can be examined as individual as well as collective through projects of identity. I would add that this agential relation is brought to the table as struggle for coherence, and continuity in the work goes on no matter what.

To be clear, I also maintain and reiterate that as a new materialist, cultural space is not defined as around and between objects. It is considered already embedded in these objects (the human–non-human), spaces and things, as well as in spacetimemattering[11]; it is diffractively working and conceptualizing difference through a spectrum of sound phenomena where home is a mutual relation of things and bodies inclusive of diverse participatory powers. As Barad insists, "the acting human subject and the known object are not separate, but entangled."[12] From an ethico-political perspective (with whom and for whom), this relational process (re)models our interdependence with human and nonhuman others, beginning with thinking and acting 'from the middle out' without discrediting the consideration for collectivity and the other.

What emerges from this conceptual relation of the artwork is making the materiality of women's work visible as a performative mode of domestic bodily production: the implicit body of a woman at work is expressed in a resonant sonic overture of resistance. A Public Kitchen is an immersive sculptural installation that is at once a multisensory, embodied, participatory encounter that engenders a mixture of feelings and visual impressions for the participants, such as fascination, surprise, boredom, disgust, perplexity, irritation, joy, and ambiguity. I argue that a Public Kitchen produces noisy affects that can contribute to transforming our social imaginations, forming daring narratives (or sonic recipes) that feed post-human ethical practices and inquiry.

4. Co-Composing the Sonic Intra-Face of a Noisy Kitchen through the Apparatus

It is a profoundly intertwined collective moment as both human and non-human elements intra-act within the apparatus. The apparatus can be seen as the framework for the social artwork: a sculptural set-up consisting of the motherboard—a long metallic platform resembling a community kitchen table used for 'placemats' of positioned kitchen tools, electric kitchen appliances and electronic music hardware. Kitchen tools and appliances are amplified and activated through the simple technology of a contact microphone, connected to the metal motherboard. A contact microphone, also known as a pickup or a piezo, is a form of microphone that senses audio vibrations through contact with solid objects and musical hardware. Thus, the transduction produced when kitchen tools interact with this active metal surface generates noise, or diffractive interference patterns, through a piezo electric effect that measures sonic vibration, pressure, acceleration, and the force which converts sound to an electrical signal. As Barad explains, "apparatuses are not mere observing instruments but boundary-drawing practices—specific material (re)configurings of the world which come to matter" (Barad 2007, p. 140). Thus, I use the apparatus as a central concept for what I argue is a new materialist approach, by working with a cluster of participants who collaborate through sound improvisation in performative intra-actions/s via the motherboard to channels of audio-electronic processing. I interpret the apparatus as a middling point for how sound performance reflects the current post-human condition and further feminist concerns. A Public Kitchen does not necessarily look high-tech when performing with kitchen tools and appliances relational to the everyday through the 'doing and cooking'; it is more about creating a condition in the installation that is a Public Kitchen—to generate a state of being for the non-human and performs in a particular temporality in relation to spacetimemattering.

---

[11] In this research, "timespacemattering" refers to how intra-actions emerge between space/time/matter relations and forces within the entanglement of differential relations (Barad 2003).
[12] (Barad 2007).

5. (Re)configuring our Relationship with the World in Co-Becoming Processes

Relationally, feminist power relations are located within the live enactment. In contributing to social change, I argue that activating a feminist ethico-politic must fundamentally emerge from work done at the transformative, energetic layer of the body, activated by doing-making processes. Cooking. Playing. Making art. Resting. Working. Sharing touch. Sharing food. Gathering to remember. Growing up. Growing old. Grieving loss and oppression. Resisting. Empowering humans. Performing ritual after ritual as an affirmative politic in action. All of these processes (and more) could be seen to fall into the 'doing-making' constellation.

(Re)configuring our relationship with the world is not a direct, elementary trajectory; it can entail messy and disquieting encounters, which embrace the indeterminate and manifest through negotiation and contradicting emotions. By engaging attentively with a sonic performance installation, a Public Kitchen entangles performers to participate in co-becoming processes, defined by Rosi Braidotti as "a co-operation of active laboring, becoming-ethical" (Braidotti and Hlavajova 2018). The challenge is to change our assumptions about the social structures that shape the world around us and take a deeply critical look at how one actually engages with the very systems that we are trying to release ourselves from, disengage, disentangle. I argue for the need to be brave and name, identify, call out, bring up, and sound out the social patterns that surround us through a sonic recipe, shifting the social dynamics we are entangled in. I argue that these social patterns of sonic textures, both tonal and atonal, maintain a quality or character of *becoming* that can be observed as other-worldly and decorous, by cultivating the experience, or can even result in disillusionment in the active process. "Becoming" here refers to feminist theoretician in new materialism, Rosi Braidotti's idea of it as a rhizomatic political action (as in, rhizomatic learning), proposing that it is a significant undertaking of nomadic feminist ethics in which transformation is to consider a body's potential for mapping and shaping transformation in the local. In turn, Braidotti considers that new futures need to be imagined first and re-assembled elsewhere in order to do *the work*, rather than being constructed into the same hierarchical frameworks.[13]

A feminist politic expands on Fluxus precedents through the use of props, costumes and makeup to create different personae with participants in a Public Kitchen: It is commonplace for performers to be adorned in crocheted masks, A-line dresses made from reflective industrial fabrics, and sticky neon duct-tape overlays. A Fluxus attitude can mean that everything that is material matter, in mind and body, is embraced—from absurd to commonplace, from violent to tedious—to ignite the kitchen space as a site that shifts and repositions its domestic status to a site of materialist agency. For example, the performance art collective, W.W.K.A. (Women with Kitchen Appliances), which existed in Montreal, Canada, from 1991 to 2013, modelled a feminist performance art approach that adhered to aesthetic concerns associated with beauty, free play and feminist autonomy. With the emergence of a Public Kitchen as a speculative and somatic proposition, and creation of a sound performance collective named Sonic Electric (currently positioned in Melbourne, Australia), a more political cultural affective reading of today's feminist discourse, conditioned by our current socio-political climate, is active through an ethico-political practice.

6. The Sonic Intra-Face of a Noisy Kitchen Workshop

How can collaborative sonic art work create a Public Kitchen (as in Figure 1)? On this collective journey, sonic material phenomena are created with kitchen tools and electric appliances, co-composed by volunteer participants who are gathered around an immersive kitchen table installation, *the motherboard*. As previously described, the motherboard is an ambulatory surface platform, resembling a lengthy metal kitchen table, that is used for the placement of kitchen tools, electric kitchen appliances and electronic music hardware. It is a vital and central component of a Public Kitchen

---

[13] (Braidotti 2002).

sculptural installation. The sonic performance installation is built on a critical arrangement of hybrid personae (costumed participants) whose bodily capacities are measured by the continuous mutual transformations between 'humans at work,' seeking to reposition the kitchen tool or appliance by exploring its displacement and functionality through the labored body (Figure 2).

Figure 1. A Public Kitchen performed by Sonic Electric at MARS Gallery, Melbourne, Australia, 2019.

Figure 2. A participant of a Public Kitchen performing in *The Future is Female* exhibition, Abbotsford Convent, Melbourne, Australia, 2018.

I argue that investigating sonic materiality through the prism of a Public Kitchen enables the power of sound performance to be activated as a savoring of self-emancipation for the participant. Sonic phenomena re-sounds from one kitchen tool to another—from Australia, Spain, Iceland and Hong Kong—through space, agency, resonance and temporality in the apparatus.[14] All of these critical attributes reverberate in Public Kitchens as socio-cultural phenomena that create points of resistance (Figure 3).

Figure 3. Participants of the 22nd International Symposium on Electronic Art. *ISEA2016 Hong Kong* 香港 *Cultural R>evolution*. Public Kitchen. School of Creative Media, City University of Hong Kong, China, 2016.

This awareness is found through a Public Kitchen, with the desire to affect what we seek to change in the entanglement, drawing people of all shapes, sizes, ages, and abilities to understand and measure difference through the feel, flow or vitality of the enactment of sonic intra-actions. This immanent process produces intra-actions and/or fluxes and vibrations of matter, resonating with human and non-human bodies. I argue for a performative feminist materialist ontology/epistemology, which sees social phenomena as primary and non-binary; here, subjects and objects are dependent on forming in or out of a process of intra-action by rethinking the dualisms so central to post-human thinking. The oppositions between nature and culture, matter and mind, the human and the non-human, are produced and combined in the action itself, reflecting on the philosophical writings of Karen Barad (2007) and Rosi Braidotti (2013).

This perspective opens up a capability for deep listening by the participants that makes them available and receptive to a tuning of the world we live in. Resonance can be seen as proposing a new way of thinking about causality and agency that acknowledges the indeterminate possibilities for worldly (re)configurings—a (re)-tuning of the world. Resonance, I would also argue, should be understood in terms of relation: a vibration that emerges out of intra-activity. This raises an awareness of the complexities involved with diffractive paradoxes revealed in sonic relations.

---

[14] The public iterations in specific localities in and around: Melbourne (Australia), Blanca (Spain), Reykjavik (Iceland), and Hong Kong (China) are all part of PhD field research work conducted from 2015 to 2019 and supported by The Victorian College of the Arts, University of Melbourne, Australia.

There are diffractive readings in making sound—or, sounding and hearing—where sound/noise resonates in composition through communication between participants: noisiness, the Public Kitchen activity, pronounces a form of resistance or critical engagement with the world. This relation also punctuates the entanglement between noise and a politics of consent in the way a diverse range of femme, female-identified and gender non-binary persons collaborate. A Public Kitchen addresses all cybernetic bodies as forms of noise and disruption that are engaged in a thinking about freedom where the mind/body is a driving force within a multiplicity of becomings; this is emphasized and expanded on through the writings of Braidotti, Gilles Deleuze and Felix Guattari (Braidotti 2013; Deleuze et al. 1987).

Understanding the Transducer

Sound patterns as sonic recipes in a Public Kitchen are formed by human participation with the help of a small electronic audio device—the contact microphone (Figure 4). Contact microphones create live contact with kitchen tools and appliances entangled within the apparatus through the motherboard. Lead cables connected to contact microphones feed guitar amplifiers placed under the motherboard, amplifying noisy material into a public space, and leading the listener on a sonic journey. It is a haptic partnership with musical hardware and bodily production that, in concert, produces sonic performative phenomena. I argue, as a multi-media visual artist, that the strength of sonic phenomena is that it does not strive to be technically perfect, musically high-tech, or audio-efficient. Instead, it accepts its place as indeterminate, vital, resonant material, celebrating its flexibility to jump from manual labored sound to electronic sonic space, and vice versa, in a sonic recipe. There are constant exchanges and transformations happening in every kitchen: forces shifting; particles entangling with particles in the quantum field of thinking; doing and making in the world in paraphrasing Barad to explain things on a molecular level (Barad 2007). These intra-actions are technologically entangled with musical hardware, constructed with industrial metal parts. Music hardware is mechanical objects or electronic devices that create, or aid in the creation of, experimental musical sounds that a musician might use to enhance *sonic material phenomena* in a live performance.

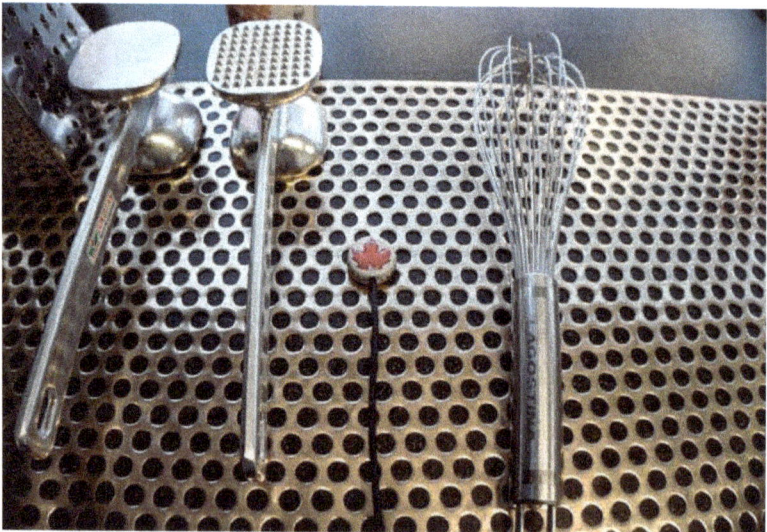

Figure 4. A contact microphone placed on the motherboard surrounded by kitchen tools. Testing Grounds, Southbank Arts Centre, Melbourne, Australia. From the sound performance work, *Being in Time: Death by Audio*, 2018.

A Public Kitchen dares to take the risks proposed by Braidotti in this paper's opening quote, as it reflects on the uncertainty of our current times to expose social rifts and find affirmative human–non-human connections in co-composing sound patterns into sonic recipes. The material realities of women's everyday lives are reflected in a Public Kitchen as, historically, we can see the kitchen as a place that separated people, as a place of oppression, a key site where women perform most of the world's labor (International Labour Organization 2016).

7. All Art Is Political

Materialities are never neutral. Thus, a Public Kitchen could be conceived as an alternative economy critical of a capitalist system. I argue that all art is political because a critical feminist perspective articulates that patriarchal culture is a system that impacts everyone as material conditions of all sorts play a vital role in sonic resistance against domination. Domination in today's cultural politics takes various forms in varying social contexts.[15]

As explained by Rosemary Hennessy, materialist feminism considers how women and men of various races and ethnicities are kept in their lower economic status due to a power imbalance that privileges those who already have privilege, thereby protecting the status quo (Hennessy and Ingraham 1997). A Public Kitchen challenges this propositionally, as it manifests a (re)building of community in the form of collective action that is unyielding through sonic material resistance, playing out as a collective pathway of negotiation and co-operation (Figure 5). This position excludes a Marxist agenda in a Public Kitchen by recognizing the agency of biology or matter in worldly phenomena and social and political human behavior. Feminist new materialists challenge the linear models of causation that form constructivist analyses of the ways power relations shape the subjects and objects of knowledge. This occupation accounts for how intra-actions through which the social, the biological, and the physical emerge, persist, and transform. Feminist new materialists are qualitatively trying to change feminist critical analysis from a framework within which the agency of bodies and material objects is understood as an effect of power to a framework within which relationally, nature-culture and biology have reciprocal agentive effects upon one another. In this material turn of the distinctive and effective agency of organisms, ecosystems, the human non-human as vital matter, feminists will rethink how to take on social justice, creating paths toward social and political transformation.

Relationally, the monotone video work, *Las Atrevidas: The Risk Takers* (2015), monitors the mechanical movements of six senior women from a small village in Blanca, Murcia, Spain, who embrace tradition, a nomadic culture through difference, and, via their participation, generate a space of subjective individuation and otherness (Figure 6). I investigate how kitchen tools are passed on socially and somatically, stretching entanglements with shifting measurements of performative movement, sonic undulations, historical kitchen knowledge, and female genealogies in the domestic sphere. I argue that, for feminists like myself, temporality exists by how time is being kept, by whom and for whom in a Public Kitchen (van der Tuin 2015). The entanglement of "doing-cooking" transfigures, as Braidotti specifies, how objects resonate as matter that thinks and feels as an extension of the human body through the post-human (Braidotti 2013). The relationship between subject and object opens complex nets of intra-connectivity in which the body, space and psyche are never conclusive and always "more than" something: as Erin Manning explains, they are "indeterminate" (Manning 2016, p. 14). A Public Kitchen presents how this awareness of kitchen objects, disciplines

---

[15] This idea points to a "Trumpian" autocrat world, such as heteropatriarchal domination, that is, a socio-political system in which the male gender and heterosexuality have primacy over other genders and over other sexual orientations, neoliberal domination, racist domination, and homophobic domination, etc. Donald John Trump is the 45th and current president of the United States of America, who took office in January 2017. "Trumpian" is a slang definition found here: https://www.dictionary.com/e/slang/trumpian/ (LLC 2019).

and practice are always operating in relation to matter that is waiting to be interpreted, rehearsed, repositioned, and transmitted (Barad 2003).

Figure 5. The local sound performance collective, Sonic Electric, performing in *The Future is Female*, Abbotsford Convent, Melbourne, Australia, 2018.

Figure 6. *Las Atrevidas: The Risk Takers*, Artist Residency at Centro Negra AADK, Blanca, Murcia, Spain, 2015. Group portrait. Video: duration 10 min.

The practice of deep listening gives women an opportunity to explore their/our bodies and their/our temporalities from women's experience as women while also being inclusive of gender-fluidity. Deep listening is also termed somatic listening by Pauline Oliveros, who observed that the practice of deep listening is a commitment to cultivating receptivity through the body with an emphasis on inclusiveness of performing music.[16] Everyone (women, men, non-binary, trans, gender fluid etc.) is engaged as participants in this practice before even touching a contact microphone. For the participant, inclusion promotes a veritable, personal movement of a thought and listening practice that helps the body unwind while at the same time stimulating awareness of energy flows of the body, quite similar to a Tai-Chi or Qigong class that incorporates Chinese medicine and the flow of chi (energy) points throughout the body. In the company of others, this approach prepares a participant foremost to listening in synchronicity with each other in performance, relational to the whole apparatus of doing-cooking as an unfolding immanent process.

Feminism today is a worldview that includes men, demanding a rethinking of power in society, a change in the dominant system of private domestic space, public space and temporality; negotiating a woman's place in art institutions and valuing a woman's place in this discourse (COST: European Cooperation in Science and Technology 2017).

What feminist new materialists point out is, what is in the world and what we know about things in the world cannot be considered as different things. What is in the world, what we know about things in the world are constantly shaping one another and, in the kitchen, this study of matter and meaning is, moreover, boiling over. Thus, the tools of the kitchen become agential matter in a post-human world. Post-humanists are responding to the redefinition of humanity's place in the world by both the technological and continuum in which the "human" is but one life form among many (Braidotti 2016).

8. Semiotics of the Kitchen

The socio-political oeuvre of American artist and activist, Martha Rosler (Rosler 1975), highlights her position on the artist's role within contemporary art practice, as well as her understanding of "private to political." This position affects and mentors the present understanding of the role of an artist as a feminist thinker, and this agential strategy energizes the creative move from the private, to political, to public space present in a Public Kitchen.

Rosler's seminal video and performance artwork, *Semiotics of the Kitchen* (1975), contributed to a recurring thematic during the 1970s that still serves as a critical document and historical precursor to current feminist materialist discourse and genealogies. In this work, the artist critiques women's roles in society by acting as a 'cooking show host' personality, creating an alphabet using different kitchen tools. The letters are articulated, often quite violently, in the process. Through Rosler's objective lens, the kitchen table and its environment are made visible as a platform of domestic labor: a form of maintenance work, household chore and food preparation. It is coded into a form of semiotics—a performative and gestural language—acted out through the aggressive, violent and monotone handling and manipulation of kitchen tools.

Rosler developed her own terms of performative engagement in front of the recording camera to articulate a feminist debate. And while this seminal work seemed to focus on her personal place in the world, Rosler's critique spilt beyond her 'artist's kitchen' to examine the political context and capitalistic economy of the late 1970s in the United States. However, her analysis didn't end there. Rosler was also accounting for the personal, bodily and psychological experience of being human. At the time, her semiotic approach pointed to a Marxist–feminist expression of frustration as a radical mode of feminist critique in that it stirred the global soup of women's oppression. Rosler's message was not only directed to the women (the Other) through which feminism defines itself, but also to the forces of government in an advanced industrial society (Molesworth 2000).

---

[16] (Oliveros 1973).

Semiotics of the Kitchen politicized the space of the kitchen through the lens of the camera, exposing issues of consumer culture, mechanized labor and material handling as a monotone assembly line. Through performance art, Rosler was steadfast in taking a stand on government in which political authority exercises absolute and centralized control through consumer capitalism. Her work has influenced the embodiment of physical labor in the kitchen and speaks especially to a Public Kitchen model, highlighting how politics and the performative can be embedded in the very material presence of video art and an alternative politics of connection. At its very center is the materiality of artistic and political action. It shows how artists can navigate this territory, giving attention to the question of politics from the perspective of theory and the artwork itself (Nicholson and Seidman 1995). This noisy platform resonates to enable the dictum that "all art is political." In the last decade, there has been a series of incremental shifts to artworks that primarily utilize forms of collaboration and participation on the ground and as live art forms. From a feminist new materialist view, physical labor is highlighted to create a form of resistance or post-human critical engagement with the world; however, the actual power of kitchen tools and appliances to create sound material to connect and contribute to the feminist discursive can build on Rosler's original ideas.

Critical reaction to collaborative practices of social engagement is always problematic in the way it is contextualized by Rosler's socio-political stand, for example. Rosler has consistently made me think of the potential to be had in developing an ethics of engagement in relation to feminist collaborative art practices. Sonic artwork can materialize in form and in practice, with such simple tools connected to electronic media and to the familiar environment around us. As a method of social engagement, a Public Kitchen seeks to create a form of creative occupation, moving from the kitchen into a public space, to create other types of kitchen environments or iterations with people other than myself. The term *iteration* is used in a single execution, as of a set of instructions that are to be repeated in a performance work. As a diffractive reading, performative gesture and the semiotic language have been extended beyond Rosler's seminal work. The kitchen table shifts in time, space and location. Each kitchen tool and appliance that is placed on the kitchen table surfaces from a set of distinct kitchen tools and skills. Each tool is picked up and transformed in live performance to become a sound instrument in its engagement with electronic media, not only with manual kitchen tools, but also with electrical modern kitchen appliances.[17] The physical body is bound up in this process (Braidotti 2002).

Therefore, a Public Kitchen shifts and repositions kitchen tools and appliances in ways that seek to open up sites of resonance and resistance. Typically, noise from the kitchen is considered unwanted—it is something extra and excessive. What is considered noise or information in human terms is seemingly processed by digital technology in an equally blank way; a problematic appearance that can hide human accountability behind the apparent autonomy of technology. This paper considers this posturing through the way communication is made noisy, and by addressing all cybernetic bodies as forms of noise and disruption that are engaged in thinking about freedom with the mind/body as a driving force with a multiplicity of becomings (Braidotti 2002, 2013).

Braidotti calls this interaction a transmutation—a qualitative change, a metamorphoses—"towards a materialist theory of becoming" by using the power of technology in an affirmative way (Braidotti 2002, p. 1; 2013, p. 21). And, like Rosler's strategy, physical labor remains an extension of the self (the participant), except now there is more than one person occupying the space at the kitchen table as collective affirmative action becomes a platform for collective, cross-disciplinary inquiry for both art and social commitment.

---

[17] It is important to pinpoint the probability of coming across unusual kitchen tools that are kitchen staples in the country from which the iteration takes place, and to distinguish the variety of different kitchen tools that are used in a Public Kitchen across the motherboard. Each kitchen tool is best used for certain foods with respect to ethnicity and locality, and the importance of using specific utensils is a guide to the gestural technique that is used by the participant.

Bodily Encounter

In Rosler's *Semiotics of the Kitchen*, the performer weaves a personal, psychic and physical encounter into the narrative. This individual encounter is critical in the handling and manipulation of kitchen tools and appliances used in food preparation, domestic labor and maintenance work to manifest a political public artwork. Rosler's artwork was explicit in her black and white, severe characterization, set in her kitchen in Brooklyn, New York. Rosler posed in front of the camera as a homemaker, picking up a kitchen tool for each letter of the alphabet and naming each tool with a violent gesture while staring, deadpan, into the video camera. At the time, the creative phenomenon of Julia Child[18] was appearing on local public television channel, PBS. Rosler, starring in her own reality cooking show in the space of her own kitchen, demonstrates the object's potential, not its culinary purpose (Figures 7 and 8).

Figure 7. Martha Rosler, *Semiotics of the Kitchen*, 1975, video, Video Data Bank, USA.

Figure 8. Julia Child in *The French Chef* on WGBH, 1963–66. Photo: Paul Child/PBS television, New York, USA.

As Julia Child so often presented through her TV personality, a kitchen tool was usually handled with skillful culinary expertise; but Rosler's deliberate physical gestures were adamant, violent and rebellious. Rosler stabbed at the air with a knife and fork as she cast off ingredients behind her into the void of the kitchen and beyond. Rosler returned her gaze to the camera lens as a mad housewife, not quite the elegant French chef.

---

[18] Julia Child revolutionized American cuisine through her PBS television cooking shows, such as *The French Chef*, *Cooking with Master Chef*, etc. Her videos are available online.

Rosler's subversive projection of a woman's place in the world signified a desire for resistance and change. However, it also signaled failure, as the artist portrayed herself as a prisoner of her own domesticity by mocking Julia Child's persona. Fast forward. In a Public Kitchen, the performer also adopts a persona. However, foremost, the aim is to underscore the role of the participant as a sound maker, a collaborator, to create sound patterns that can resonate as a social and political marker for resistance and change but can also signal the failure not to do so. The sound material that is collected will be variable. Its indeterminate pathway will either fail or succeed in its outcome and potentiality.

Semiotics of the Kitchen is testament to today's continued addiction to entertainment in the form of cooking shows and the world of celebrity chefs. Television media has amplified the artifice by which social media and the power of television homogenizes and distracts from meaningful social action. Rosler employed parody in the way that cooking shows inhabit our screen and social consciousness: she deconstructed gender, tracing how feminist genealogy pays particular attention to discourses, bodies and power. In a Public Kitchen dynamic, the participant is encouraged to engage in over-the-top theatricality, or to mask psychological or emotional identification. In this way, they play out, as Rosler did, with deadpan humor and passive aggression in order to reflect society's pull of conformity and homogenization.

9. Resistance through Noisy Resonance

> "Drama is very important in life: You have to come on with a bang. You never want to go out with a whimper." (Julia Child to Jacques Pepin during *Cooking in Concert* television program (Child and Pepin 1996).

Noisy resonance emerges at a vibration of larger amplitude when produced by all participants playing a kitchen appliance in a sonic recipe. It is this noisy crescendo that fills the space of a Public Kitchen. Materially, it becomes a resonating system of vibrational bodies inclusive of a kitchen object's interference patterns. Resonance, scientifically and acoustically, occurs when a system preferentially vibrates at a certain frequency. This frequency is called resonant frequency, and the system will respond very strongly to any periodic force at that frequency. The exact frequencies at which objects resonate is largely determined by the object's physical properties: its size, shape and the materials that it's made out of. Many objects have resonant frequencies, and they are the source of many of the sounds we hear. When you knock on something, much of the sound you hear is just the ringing of that object's resonance. Even our own bodies have many (Pyzdek 2018).

Sound resonates through human sensory behavior experience by sculpting, shifting and changing the perception in which the body labors to listen creatively to objects and other bodies vibrating; this process is critical of power relations in the kitchen environment. A field of resonance is important to me in the material discursive and the transversal[19] (Rhoades and Brunner 2010). Resonance strikes a chord in a Public Kitchen in the act of reclaiming thought or sound which is important for feminism, new materialism and my own practice. Sound, relationally, works its way to the forefront of contemporary sensory behavior and user experience by sculpting, shifting and changing our perception of the kitchen environment in which the body labors to listen creatively and critically.

In new materialist thinking, resonance can replace the binaries of structuralist thought, shedding new light on contemporary debates between sound, aurality, cognition, subjectivity, and embodiment. I argue that this is due to resonance's ability to dissolve the binary of the materiality of things (human-non-human), and compels us to call into question that something, such as resonance, must therefore situate itself as a form of resounding together in the discourse of post-humanism and other

---

[19] Transversality addresses different existential territories and universes of value through the register of resonance. (Guattari 2003). "Psychanalyse et transversalité". Paris: Maspero/La Découverte. "Transversal Fields of Experience" brings different points of entry into resonance that all revolve around the question of how we open up new registers that incite a creative moving with the forces we encounter in contemporary transversal fields that shape our everyday experiences (Rhoades and Brunner 2010).

immersive feminist participatory practices. For many feminists and artists alike, labor relations and ecological issues become more crucial to our survival every day. In a Public Kitchen, I see sonic connections of shared affective and productive movement to understand new material physicalities, new emotional transformations and new sonic relations, intra-culturally, with others and the world. A Public Kitchen takes affirmative action into the streets as a form of resonance. The kitchen object is relational, in that is has the capacity to make felt how an object is already in a field of relation and tuning through intra-action, intensities and symbolic forces of resonance. A feminist new materialist position illuminates a cartography and radical visibility for challenging theoretical concepts of art and everyday life, work and value for individuals, women, communities, and women's oppression in the global environment.

Therefore, it is important to discuss or consider the ways in which different discourses, such as affect, mingle with matter and virtuality in the kitchen. Through this discussion of the artwork of Rosler and her social-political connection to the materialization of the labored body, as well as my critique of a Public Kitchen, I aim to find a modulation, or flow, of affect in the discursive that never jumps clear of its entanglement in the processes of new materialist performativity. Instead, it assists in unpacking and defining resonance and power relations, enhancing the position of feminist genealogies.

Working on transnational participatory collaboration is a real process demanding particular concepts and commitments. Teaching sound through deep listening is a practice. Creating a visual aesthetic of performativity within the immersive assemblage is also significant. The entanglement of bodies and the sound that is transmitted, are foregrounded in a resonant system. Through this process and apparatus, it becomes clear that what is transcended through sound is the understanding that the enactment is re-arranged with every iteration and is always evolving.

Contact microphones and electronic media move in the mind, through the body and through things as resonance is heightened, and, as Manning characterizes, develop into something "more than" movement: "It is out of time, untimely, rhythmically inventing its own pulse" (Manning 2016, p. 2). Thus, a sonic performance work makes public the sound material that is emitted from kitchen objects—a new materialist way of listening and behaving, not *in* but *of* the resonant world.

From Failure to Empowerment

American artist, Mierle Laderman Ukeles, writes in her exhibition proposal, "Manifesto for Maintenance Art, 1969! Proposal for an Exhibition CARE", that "Maintenance is a drag," confirming that maintenance is unglamorous, tedious, hard work and economically underestimated (Ukeles 1969). In a not-so-perfect world, something is always breaking, wearing down, getting dirty or falling apart. In the performance, this lopsidedness and inequality is transmitted as an embedded and entangled process of coming into, working through, being formed by, and forming something into a sound recipe—a set of sound patterns created by participants. The unevenness of this process in sound and noise art is relevant to how the participants, at times, are almost failing at getting the object to make a sound or trying to change how the object can be rendered mute/useless in its repositioning. The sound, as a physical phenomenon, is transduced into an excited state, becoming dynamic as it is electrified, as contact is made with an electronic contact microphone. When the contact microphone is removed or disconnected, the object returns to its static self again. This is a complex relationship where human, non-human and so many natural, social, political, and cultural factors are forces that resonate in the entangled processes of materialization. Surely 'failure' is recognized as agential forces that activate an acknowledgement of nature, the body and materiality in matters of uncertainty—indeterminacy within the intra-action? This failure slippage plays simultaneously into the timeline, where indeterminacy of position and momentum in the sonic compositional arrangement manifests as a communication breakdown. It appears, within each diffractive reading, as a disconnect, or simply the object responding in an auditory relation as if it is being agitated in the failure to produce a resonance, or keep going, or fade away.

I would shape this disruptive mode of engagement in consciousness and thought as creating resonant agitation with kitchen objects in the radical potential of the political. This agitation is defined by a discomposure or disturbance that is transmitted through resonance, such as through the delivery of a feminist manifesto. To me, agitating space with sound and noise art demands a new way of understanding participatory practice, audience perception and difference in manners of expression and modes of experience of the artwork.

Akin to Rosler, I lived in New York City during the 1970s and was exposed to performance art, punk and hard-core music, which were important influences for many local artists. Girl power, or GRRRL power, acknowledged a woman's space in the world of music and the performing arts.[20] The Riot Grrrl subculture emerged in the early 1990s from the punk rock scene during the third-wave feminist movement, uniting women and girls against capitalist and patriarchal cultural ideologies. Countering the dominant ideological narrative in the United States, the Riot Grrrl movement continues to evolve and expand to avoid commodification. Moving between high and low art, the relevance of *sound as social* with feminist and political concerns and polarities is activated in a Public Kitchen through a bricolage of incongruent cultural elements that become ripe for exploitation.[21] This attitude was rampant in New York City from as far back as the birth of Happenings on the Lower East Side in the 1980s, and the subsequent significant and pugnacious punk and hardcore scenes. Rosler may have taken note of this local scene, as many of these bands had humorous elements to them. The performers dressed in ludicrous outfits, engaged in slapstick routines and experimented with different styles of experimental noise-making. The desire to create music with different tools demonstrates John Cage's celebration of noise and accident (Cage 1961); it is also informative to note that he was teaching at the New School in New York during this time. This methodology refers to putting sounds together in a random, indeterminate manner; mixing and matching unrelated sounds, noises and breakages in performance.

It was this very combination of moving between musical styles and art practices that led to a productive cross-fertilization between music and art, not only in New York and London, but subsequently in Berlin in the 1980s and beyond. By using a non-musical interface, new expressions were generated. A Fluxus attitude of the 1960s reflected performers dressed in these beforementioned ludicrous outfits, engaging in slapstick routines and experimenting with different styles of noise-making to attract attention to what was happening on the streets and in social life (O'Dell 1997, p. 41) (Figure 9).

Lunacy is an interesting word in contemporary ethico-political discourse. It takes special skills to perform and participate in performative politics today in a "Trumpian" world of conspiracy theory, gas lighting and fake news being a coercer in enabling alt-right rhetorical propaganda.[22] Lunacy is the new norm, responding to the political climate, serving up more dead-pan humor. For example, a performative pandemonium recently played out at the White House, Capitol building in the USA on 5 September 2018. A much-anticipated hearing of Judge Brett Kavanaugh's Supreme Court confirmation before the Senate Judiciary Committee was stalled by mostly feminist activists: In particular, they were protesting Kavanaugh's nomination due to his conservative stance on abortion. Outside the hearing room, female activists dressed as characters from *The Handmaid's Tale* (2017)—an American dystopian drama web television series created by Bruce Miller, based on the 1985 novel of the same name by Canadian writer, Margaret Atwood (Miller 2017). Inside, more than 70 protestors were arrested for yelling and disrupting the proceedings. It was probably the most confrontational Supreme Court (SCOTUS) nomination hearing in recent memory. I would arguably call it a performance art act using

---

[20] "GRRRL" is a slogan that encourages and celebrates women's empowerment, independence, and confidence. The slogan's invention is credited to US punk band, Bikini Kill, who published a zine called *Girl Power* in 1991.

[21] The Swiss artist, Christian Marclay, has acknowledged that during the Fluxus years he was also influenced by the ridicule of, and play on, the formal presentation of music in the concert setting and the live act (Kelly 2009, p. 151).

[22] lunacy (as in "folly") n.: foolish or senseless behavior. 2018. *Nisus Thesaurus*. Princeton: Princeton University Library. Gaslighting is a form of psychological manipulation that seeks to sow seeds of doubt in a targeted individual or in members of a targeted group, making them question their own memory, perception, and sanity.

affective political affirmative tactics. I would also posit what Braidotti distinguishes as "a break with the *doxa*": the acquiescent application of established norms and values by de-territorializing them and introducing an alternative ethic flow (Braidotti and Hlavajova 2018, p. 224).

Figure 9. Sonic Electric sound performance collective led and choreographed by Juliana España Keller 2019.

There is a dangerous seduction in picking up kitchen tools dressed as hybrid personas. This experience develops an understanding of the many facets of ourselves, thus enabling personal transformation, social dissonance and sonic resonance (Figure 10). There is truth to playing in unity, expanding on *all that matters* There is political power in the participants' participatory position within a feminist group collective that is played out through the Public Kitchen. Many artist participants would agree to meddling with conceptual standards against which political performative art playfully pushes. As each participant dons a synthetic wig or a crocheted facial mask, the body is the mind in this assumed persona. A dissociation from Cartesian mind-body thinking is also heightened because it breaks down gender barriers as much as it reinforces an idea that you put on a gender, like a change of clothing, immune to utopic thinking. As the punk movement grew out of a drab and dark environment—with participants ready to challenge the status quo and show their contempt for government, society and tradition—it is amusing that the counter-culture term "punk" is now part of mainstream clothing design. Originally intended as a destruction of fashion—both at the literal level through the defacement and damaging of garments, and at the symbolic level via its anarchistic attitude and often blasphemous message—this form of dystopic dressing up enables a sense of freedom and relief to those who participate in a Public Kitchen iteration.

This performative approach can be looked upon as a quantum thinking response[23], not only to what we want in the live performance but who we are being, shattering boundaries between mind and

---

[23] According to Barad, the deeply connected way that everything is entangled with everything else means that any act of observation makes a "cut" between what is included and excluded from what is being considered (Barad 2007, p. 175).

body. The earliest iterations of performance art, tinged in nihilism (the Dada movement, for example), flirted with the anarchic meaninglessness of language in the early twentieth century (Cohn 2008). The Futurists developed a rowdy theatrical tradition of declamation and noisy musical accompaniment (Cohn 2008). A feminist political rancor is a communal heartache demonstrating the noisy politics of everyone's oppression. The inventory of kitchen tools and appliances of a participant's choice, some from their own kitchen, are placed in front of them. It is as if a cacophonic supper of a specific recipe from a TV cooking show is about to be prepared, but this time it assumes a dystopic fervor, similar to the one witnessed in *The Handmaid's Tale* (2017). It becomes a noisy spectacle of human locomotion, of bodies made into objects extended by a sonic apparatus.

Figure 10. A participant of the group, Sonic Electric, re-positioning a flour sifter in a Public Kitchen, 2019.

10. Conclusions

A sonic performative live art experience is never fully translatable and has the potential to articulate many perspectives. I conclude that the nature of sound performance art can be articulated as both metaphysical and material. Sound performance needs to be heard to be experienced because there will always be a surplus of sonic meaning and affect which defies containment in any medium other than the sound itself. I maintain that a Public Kitchen is a live interpretation of the social experience of a sound performance artwork. In this interpretation: human machine learning, automation, representation, and uncanny choreographies oscillate between humans, diffractively, with the complexity of mechanical gestures of the somatic body. I use speculative processes, partnered with material phenomena, chemical and physical forces, and intensities, to magnify time-based acts such as sound performance in both research and practice. In this paper, or in a Public Kitchen, I track movement between the human and non-human through intra-actions of the labored body: this is done by emphasizing dramatic transformation as a new materialist politic of connection in a post-human world and future social robotics as a platform for collective, transdisciplinary inquiry for art and social action and a way of understanding the world from within, as a middling, as much as a part of it.

It is challenging to move nomadically. The entanglement with new materialism, and the engagement in post-humanist thought raises the stakes in the ethico-political consideration of the paths we should consider taking as a species through feminist participatory practices. The artwork, in relation to performative art practices and research-creations offers something more in the arena of public debate and pedagogical practices and makes ordinary participants capable of creating and transforming their own world through a freedom that is distributed individually or by the collective interpretation and practice of a sonic performance. This situated knowledge is critical, creating a rhizomatic relationship between the personal and the collective, validating authentic traditional kitchen tool knowledge around doing-cooking. Somatic learning makes the unconscious conscious, and in the process, leaves one with more options for moving, acting, thinking, and living. It maximizes not just the physical body but one's full human potential.

To reiterate, Braidotti asserts that a philosophy of the body is long overdue in the humanities to address women, gender, critical race, science, media, culture, and animals despite all the clichés we have in mind about femininity or feminism and transdisciplinary practices. I propose that I attend to difference, diffraction, and affect in knowledge production and feminist thought, intensities, emotions and somatic gestures, always being open to the more-than human towards a feminist ethico-politic. I argue the artwork forms a rupture, a collapse in the everyday making of semiotic codes permissible in the performing (the doing-cooking with kitchen tools) in the kitchen in a processual context and works hard for social justice.

A sonic recipe does not fix the post-human world but creates a noisy culture of social (re)imagining. It is a becoming of being, entangled in things and technologies, contributing to feminist genealogies and ethico-political practices. Our bodies depend on food from, in, and through the world of a kitchen environment, and our societies are built on and through things such as kitchen tools and appliances. This is how a Public Kitchen thrives.

Funding: This research received no external funding.

Conflicts of Interest: The author declares no conflict of interest.

References

Barad, Karen. 2003. Posthumanist Performativity: Toward an Understanding of How Matter Comes to Matter. *Signs* 28: 801–31. [CrossRef]
Barad, Karen. 2007. *Meeting the Universe Halfway: Quantum Physics and the Entanglement of Matter and Meaning.* Durham: Duke University Press.
Braidotti, Rosi. 2002. *Metamorphoses: Towards a Materialist Theory of Becoming.* Cambridge and Malden: Polity Press.
Braidotti, Rosi. 2013. *The Posthuman.* Cambridge and Malden: Polity Press.
Braidotti, Rosi. 2014. Conclusion: The Residual Spirituality in Critical Theory: A Case for Affirmative Postsecular Politics. In *Transformations of Religion and the Public Sphere.* New York: Palgrave Macmillan, pp. 249–72.
Braidotti, Rosi. 2016. Posthuman Feminism. Paper presented at Posthuman Feminism Conference, Melbourne, Australia, December 9.
Braidotti, Rosi, and Maria Hlavajova. 2018. *Posthuman Glossary.* London: Bloomsbury Academic.
Cage, John. 1961. *Silence: Lectures and Writings by John Cage.* Middletown: Wesleyan University Press.
Child, Julia, and Jacques Pepin. 1996. Cooking in Concert. In *PBS Food.* Edited by PBS. Boston: PBS.
Cohn, Terri. 2008. *The Art of Participation: 1950 to Now.* San Francisco: Thames & Hudson.
Conrad, Diane, and Anita Sinner. 2015. *Creating Together. Participatory, Community-Based, and Collaborative Arts Practices and Scholarship across Canada.* Waterloo: Wilfred Laurier University Press.
COST: European Cooperation in Science and Technology. 2017. *IS1307: New Materialism: Networking European Scholarship on 'How Matter Comes to Matter'.* Barcelona: COST, November 20–22.
de Certeau, Michel, Luce Giard, and Pierre Mayol. 2014. *Practice of Everyday Life: Living and Cooking.* Minneapolis: University of Minnesota Press.

Deleuze, Gilles, Felix Guattari, and Brian Massumi. 1987. *A Thousand Plateaus: Capitalism and Schizophrenia*. London and New York: Bloomsbury Academic.

Flowers, Rick, and Elaine Swan. 2011. 'Eating at Us': Representations of knowledge in the activist documentary film Food, Inc. *Studies in the Education of Adults* 43: 234–50. [CrossRef]

Guattari, Félix. 2003. *Psychanalyse et Transversalité*. Paris: Maspero/La Découverte. First published 1972.

Hennessy, Rosemary, and Chrys Ingraham. 1997. *Materialist Feminism: A Reader in Class, Difference, and Women's Lives*. New York: Routledge.

Hooks, Bell. 2000. *Where We Stand: Class Matters*. New York and London: Routledge.

Huybrechts, Liesbeth, ed. 2014. *Participation Is Risky: Approaches to Joint Creative Processes*. Amsterdam: Antennae, Valiz.

International Labour Organization. 2016. Women at Work: Trends 2016. Geneva, Switzerland. Available online: https://www.ilo.org/wcmsp5/groups/public/---dgreports/---dcomm/---publ/documents/publication/wcms_457317.pdf (accessed on 10 March 2019).

Kelly, Caleb. 2009. *Cracked Media: The Sound of Malfunction*. Cambridge: MIT Press.

Kumar, Somesh. 2002. *Methods for Community Participation. A Complete Guide for Practitioners*. New Delhi: Practical Action Publishing Ltd.

LLC. 2019. Dictionary.com. Trumpian. Available online: https://www.dictionary.com/e/slang/trumpian/ (accessed on 21 August 2019).

Lloyd, Justine, and Ellie Vasta. 2017. *Reimagining Home in the 21st Century*. Cheltenham: Edward Elgar Publishing.

Manning, Erin. 2016. *The Minor Gesture*. Durham: Duke University Press.

Manning, Erin. 2019. *How the Minor Moves Us: Across Thresholds, Socialities, and Techniques. A Conversation with Erin Manning*. Edited by Halbe Kuipers. Amsterdam: Open! Platform for Art, Culture & the Public Domain.

Massumi, Brian. 2002. *Parables for the Virtual: Movement, Affect, Sensation*. Durham: Duke University Press.

Miller, Bruce. 2017. *The Handmaid's Tale*. TV Series; Los Angeles: Hulu.

Molesworth, Helen. 2000. Cleaning Up in the 1970's: The Work of Judy Chicago, Mary Kelly and Mierle Laderman Ukeles. *October* 92: 71–97. [CrossRef]

Murphie, Andrew. 2016. *The Go-To How to Book of Anarchiving*. Montreal: The Senselab.

Nicholson, Linda, and Steven Seidman. 1995. *Social Postmodernism: Beyond Identity Politics*. New York: Cambridge University Press.

O'Dell, Kathy. 1997. Fluxus Femininus. *The Drama Review* 41: 43–61. [CrossRef]

Oliveros, Pauline. 1973. *On Sonic Meditation*. San Diego: Center for Music Experiment and Related Research, University of California, vol. 27.

Pyzdek, Andrew. 2018. The World through Sound: Resonance. Acoustics Today. Available online: https://acousticstoday.org/wts-pi/ (accessed on 10 March 2019).

Revelles-Benavente, Beatriz, and Ana M. González Ramos. 2017. *Teaching Gender. Feminist Pedagogy and Responsibility in Times of Political Crisis*. London and New York: Routledge.

Rhoades, Troy, and Christoph Brunner. 2010. "Transversal Fields of Experience" Inflexions 4, "Transversal Fields of Experience". December, pp. i–vii. Available online: www.inflexions.org (accessed on 21 August 2019).

Rosler, Martha. 1975. *Semiotics of the Kitchen*. B&W Mono. Chicago: Video Data Bank.

Strom, Kathryn J., and Adrian D. Martin. 2017. Imagination and Praxis: Criticality and Creativity in Education and Educational Research. In *Becoming-Teacher. A Rhizomatic Look at First-Year Teaching*. Rotterdam: Sense Publishers, vol. 12.

Torrens, Valentin. 2014. *How We Teach Performance Art. University Courses and Workshop Syllabus*. Denver: Outskirts Press.

Ukeles, Mierle Laderman. 1969. *Manifesto for Maintenance Art, 1969! Proposal for an Exhibition Care*. New York: Ronald Feldman Fine Arts.

van der Tuin, Iris. 2015. *Generational Feminism: New Materialist Introduction to a Generative Approach*. Lanham: Lexington Books.

 © 2019 by the author. Licensee MDPI, Basel, Switzerland. This article is an open access article distributed under the terms and conditions of the Creative Commons Attribution (CC BY) license (http://creativecommons.org/licenses/by/4.0/).

Article

Entanglements of Difference as Community Togetherness: Faith, Art and Feminism

Anna Hickey-Moody * and Marissa Willcox

Digital Ethnography Research Centre, School of Media and Communication, RMIT University, Melbourne VIC 3001, Australia; marissa.willcox@rmit.edu.au
* Correspondence: anna.hickey-moody@rmit.edu.au

Received: 14 May 2019; Accepted: 12 September 2019; Published: 18 September 2019

Abstract: Using a feminist, new materialist frame to activate ethico-political research exploring religion and gender at a community level both on Instagram and in arts workshops, we show how sharing ethnic backgrounds, religious beliefs, gender identities and sexualities through art practice entangles a diffraction of differences as 'togetherness'. Such entanglement creates cross-cultural interfaith understandings and gender diverse acceptance and inclusion online. We use diffraction, intra-action and entanglement as a way of framing our understanding of this 'togetherness' and show that human feelings rely on more-than-human assemblages; they rely on homelands, countries, wars, places of worship, orientations, attractions, aesthetics, art and objects of attachment. The feelings of 'community' and 'belonging' that we discuss are therefore direct products of human and non-human interactions, which we explore through arts-based research. In this article, we apply Karen Barad's feminist new materialist theories of 'diffraction', 'intra-action' and 'entanglement' to ways of thinking about human experience as intra-acting with aspects of the world that we classify as non-human. We use these new materialist frames to reconceptualize the human feelings of 'community', 'belonging' and 'what really matters' in feminist and intra-religious collaborative art practices and Instagram-based art communities. To better understand and encourage communities of difference, we argue that the feelings of 'community' and 'belonging', which are central to human subjectivity and experience, are produced by more-than-human assemblages and are central to identity. The methodologies we present are community focused, intra-active, arts-based research strategies for interrogating and understanding expressions of 'community' and 'belonging'. We identify how creative methods are a significant and useful way of knowing about communities and argue that they are important because they are grounded in being *with* communities, showing that the specificity of their materiality needs to be considered.

Keywords: diffraction; intra-action; entanglement; community; togetherness; faith; art; feminism; religion; belonging; methods

---

We are all humans, but some of us are just more mortal than others. (Braidotti 2013, p. 3)

Diffraction as a way of thinking draws attention to the agency of the non-human, the ways that the materials used to make art can change thinking and can change relationships between people ... building more than human relationships. Arts based practices offer an ideal way not only of accessing but also of reorganizing emotional investments. (Hickey-Moody 2018, p. 8)

1. Introduction

The feelings of 'community' and 'belonging' are products of human and non-human intra-action and enmeshment, which we explore through arts-based research. We apply the feminist new materialist concepts of 'diffraction', 'intra-action' and 'entanglement' (Barad 2007) to ways of thinking about human experience as intra-acting with aspects of the world that we classify as non-human. We use these new materialist frames to reconceptualize the human feelings of 'community', 'belonging' and 'what really matters' in feminist and intra-religious collaborative art practices and Instagram-based art communities. To better understand and encourage communities of difference, we argue that these feelings of 'community' and 'belonging' are produced by more-than-human assemblages and are central to identity. The methodologies we present are community-focused, intra-active, arts-based research strategies for interrogating and understanding expressions of 'community' and 'belonging'. We identify how live and creative methods are more than a way of *knowing* about communities, they are a way of *being entangled* with communities. As such, the specificity of their materiality needs to be considered.

According to Deleuze and Guattari "flesh is only the thermometer of a becoming" (Deleuze and Guattari 1994, p. 179), if we take this as an accurate description, which we do, then emotion is the psychological register of change and attachment. We have two similar strategies for mapping such becomings, and these articulate in different empirical projects. First, our (Hickey-Moody 2017, 2018, 2019; Hickey-Moody and Harrison 2018) methodology for working with faith communities[1] establishes new materialist approaches to qualitative visual research methods. This project fosters interfaith relationships in childhood and is designed to help communicate the ways in which communities experience belonging and togetherness through their celebration of religious differences and various cultural practices. Second, our method for working with feminist and queer Instagram artists builds on Dolphijn and van der Tuin's (2012) new materialist approach to interviewing and Les Back's (2012) 'live' sociology or live methods, to employ a method of "Instagram live interviewing" with a feminist new materialist lens. By intra-acting the interview live, we aim to understand how these artists build feminist activist communities online through their political representations of gender, feminism and sexuality. We position the agency of the interview as enmeshed with the body in space and the body in digital and virtual environments. Together, we examine the politics embedded in art making and sharing processes that allow for intersectional dialogues of inclusion to emerge through the entangled differences between bodies, cultures, religions and sexualities. We align these digital understandings and art practices with the community arts workshops that foster interfaith relations and the sharing of religious differences amongst children of different faith backgrounds, including secular children (Hickey-Moody 2018; Hickey-Moody and Harrison 2018). Our theorisation of these digital and social communities are sites for comparison and we see the creative methods used to entangle ourselves within these spaces as parallel to one another. The discussion in this paper highlights how practices of blurring the boundaries between the virtual and the real in community art practice makes way for a new materiality of communities that are based on difference. We discuss our findings in relation to understanding how the communities we engage with experience diffractions of difference as an expression of 'belonging'. We look at examples of fieldwork from both projects that amplify the significance of belonging, togetherness, acceptance and inclusion as expressed through art in both religious and newly arrived communities as well as feminist digital art groups.

We write as two white women, one of us is a Canadian migrant of post WW2 Jewish and German descent and the other a first-generation daughter of two migrants from Ireland and England who moved to Australia in their mid-twenties. Our experiences of migration and negotiating diaspora offer important points of connection when becoming with our research participants in exploring themes of home and belonging. One of us is the child of an Irish political musician and IRA sympathizer, for whom the embodied history of the Irish civil war and famine have been key to learning about the politics of colonization and problematizing relationships between religion and social/cultural power. The history of the Cromwellian Penal Laws against Catholics in Ireland, which denied education, emancipation and landownership to any Irish Catholic were not repealed until 1829 and is echoed

---

[1] Professor Anna Hickey-Moody is recipient of the Australian Research Council Future Fellowship project number FT 160100293 'Early Start Arts to Counter Radicalization' funded by the Australian Government.

in the class system in Ireland, which is shaped by a complex enmeshment of religion and geography. The close relationships between war and religion embedded in Irish history were the inspiration for part of the fieldwork discussed here, which examines relationships between religion, community and belonging. Similarly, Holocaust histories constitute the genetic material of any Jewish survivors of WW2 and their descendants. This generational trauma and attunement to a past history of conflict is a point of connection that can often be part of *becoming with* our research participants from migrant backgrounds and refugee pasts. Our places of connection in relation to gender and sexuality which is further explored in the Instagram research here are similar forms of enmeshment of difference: one of us identifies as bi-sexual and as both of us present as women, we consistently experience patriarchal and capitalist overcodings of our bodies that leave us profoundly attuned to the power of queer, decolonial feminist imagery. We share crucial points of connection with our participants and consistently look to learn from and celebrate our differences as being a form of community 'togetherness'.

Diffracting Difference

Diffractions and entanglements of matter and meaning emerge from the telling, making and drawing of visual 'migration stories' in the UK and Australia (Hickey-Moody 2018), and also in the feminist activist art we see on Instagram. The depth and diversity of the communities that we study in relation to their sense of belonging, togetherness, inclusion and acceptance is diffracted but also brought into being through art practice.

> Diffraction is not reflection raised to some higher power. It is not a self-referential glance back at oneself. While reflection has been used as a methodological tool by scholars relying on representationalism, there are good reasons to think that diffraction may serve as a productive model for thinking through nonrepresentationalist methodological approaches. (Barad 2007, p. 88)

Diffracting, or breaking apart a ray of light shows up its many components and indeed co-constructs these components in the process of diffraction. Diffraction makes in new ways, rather than mirrors. In her book chapter "Queer Causation and the Ethics of Mattering", Karen Barad (2008) re-works material from *Meeting the Universe Halfway* by applying 'diffraction' to the scientific discovery of the many light changing lenses of the brittlestar (an Ophiuroid). The brittlestar has a survival method of breaking off and losing some of its arms to distract predators. In this example, Barad positions brittlestars as being a part of this world, and this diffraction of their limbs symbolizes their entanglement with the environment. She asks,

> When is a broken-off limb only a piece of the environment and when it is an offspring? At what point does the 'disconnected' limb belong to the 'environment' rather than the 'brittlestar'? Is contiguity of body parts required in the specification of a single organism? Can we trust visual delineations to define bodily boundaries? Can we trust our eyes? Connectivity does not require physical contiguity. (Spatially separate particles in an *entangled state* do not have separate identities, but rather are part of the same phenomena.) (Barad 2008, p. 327)

In broad terms, Barad (2008) is questioning why differences, and in this case bodily diffractions, are seen as being separated from the environment when she asks "can we trust our eyes?" (p. 327). She points to the notion that connectivity does not require contiguity, therefore, though something may appear different, this does not necessarily mean that it is. Barad opposes this focus on difference by redefining the space between the brittlestar's body and the environment, its limbs are diffracted *into* the environment rather than *away from* the body. She says "the world is an ongoing intra- active engagement, and bodies are among the differential performances *of* the world's dynamic intra-activity, in an endless reconfiguring of boundaries and properties, including those of spacetime" (Barad 2008, p. 326). In our research, bodies of water, matter, flesh, soil, sand and stone are reconfigured across spacetime in contextually specific ways. Religious differences and similarities are diffracted through art making and storytelling. Stories of migration, attachment, belonging, devotion and spiritual life are shared through words, colours, pattern, paint and pictures. Colors, symbols and feelings bring bodies together, and position them on shared earth. Feminist artists create and share art on Instagram with the political aim of advancing feminist agendas on themes such as LGBTQIA+ activism, reproductive justice, self-love and body positivity. It is through this entangled set of diffractions between various modes of story-telling, art making, digital creation and discussion that we find that intersecting themes of social inclusion evolve, through the creative methods with which we employ. By using intersectional feminist modes of social inclusion, Instagram artists build online communities from their art practice and actively participate in intersectional dialogue on their Instagram pages. Kimberle Crenshaw (1989) urges researchers to focus on this 'intersectionality' by looking at the conjoining oppressions at play across structures, systems and institutions. She problematizes some feminist theory and antiracist politics because of the "focus on the most privileged group members [which] marginalizes those who are multiply-burdened and obscures claims that cannot be understood as resulting from discrete sources of discrimination" (Crenshaw 1989, p. 140). Both the children artists and feminist activist artists diffract differences between their religions, races, ethnic backgrounds, sexualities and gender identities through their art making, either in a digital timespace or collaborative community workshop. These stories of intersectional inclusion told through art are how we explore the diffraction of differences as community making.

Using a feminist new materialist frame to activate ethico-political research in religion and gender at a community level, we theorize that the sharing of ethnic backgrounds, religious beliefs, gender identities and sexualities through art practice encourages a diffraction of difference as 'togetherness' by creating interfaith understandings and inclusion of diverse bodies and sexualities online. We use diffraction, intra-action and enmeshment in framing our understanding of this 'togetherness', and as a way of showing that these feelings rely on more-than-human assemblages, they rely on homelands, countries, wars, places of worship, practices of identification and objects of attachment.

Feminist and new materialist scholarship together, demonstrates the co-implication of bodies, subjectivities, places and histories. After van der Tuin (2008), Braidotti (2013), Barad (2007), Dolphijn and van der Tuin (2012), Barrett and Bolt (2014) and more, feminist new materialism accounts for this enmeshment of the social and the material, the virtual and real, human and non-human assemblage. For feminist new materialists, matter is agentic, ever changing, unpredictable and always becoming. Many feminist new materialist scholars (Hickey-Moody 2018; Ringrose and Renold 2016) posit perspectives and methodologies using methods we build upon here, grounded in arts-practice, intra-active interviewing, and embodied underpinnings of feminist identity and community research. It is important to note the co-implicated and relational nature of matter in new materialism. This is pedagogically significant in the respect that all bodies, not just human bodies, are endowed with agency and complexity. Barad's neologism *intra-activity* allows us to see this:

> The notion of *intra-action* (in contrast to the usual "interaction," which presumes the prior existence of independent entities/relate) represents a profound conceptual shift. It is through specific agential intra-actions that the boundaries and properties of the "components" of phenomena become determinate and that particular embodied concepts become meaningful. (Barad 2003, p. 815)

Intra-activity is a concept grounded in philosophies of immanence. There is no 'beyond' the body, rather, the focus shifts to a 'between' located *in*, *with* and *through* the body, as enacted "material-discursive phenomena" (Barad 2003, p. 821). Bodies are therefore inseparable from discursive practices. New materialist theory (Barad 2007; van der Tuin 2015; Palmer 2016) suggests that we would *not be the same selves* outside the field in which we are constituted, and that through the entanglement of our research site and ourselves, *we change*, and the subjects of our research change as well. The process of being together re-makes us. An example is our art making workshops, featured in the photograph below, in which experiences of art making are entangled with the participants sharing of their backgrounds.

A philosophy of intra-action shows us that we make the data we collect, and indeed, creation is the object of the research process, rather than discovering something that is 'there' to be known. This complicates understandings of research methods and comes to show that the data which is generated and collected through fieldwork is co-created by the fieldwork assemblage. 'Data' is the residue of successful complex qualitative research processes that engage young people in collaborative making practices that call them to think together about the future, about social values and community life.

Our affective research method with Instagram live interviewing embodies the experience of being live on Instagram and being broadcast into the participants' world and online community. In Instagram live interviews, both the researcher and her interviewee sit staring at a phone screen—often necessarily positioned extremely close together, in the participant's art studio, or tattoo studio, sweating and noticing how awkward it is to stare at a screen while talking to one another. This embodied proximity, while awkward, also brings with it a relationality which is key to sharing information across the course of the interview. This online intra-action of the researcher and the participants' bodies is further explored and theorized as ethnographic observation through ethnographic fieldnotes.

Both fieldwork examples from Hickey-Moody and Willcox (2019)'s work respectively demonstrate how bodies and 'things' are not separate and shows how intra-actions are vital to how we come to know ourselves as humans and interact with our environments. Through unpacking examples from practical methods for data generation, we show the potential ways our students and research participants can be called on to relate to each other and themselves in our classrooms and interview spaces. Through diffractive and intra-active methods, we are enabled to draw upon memory, culture, religion, tradition, bodies, art and politics via methods that may be substantively different from ways people often are prompted to see themselves and relate to others in theory based learning environments or traditional research practices. As Barad (2014) reminds us, "Diffraction queers binaries and calls out for a rethinking of the notions of identity and difference" (p. 171). She continues, stating,

> The key is understanding that identity is not essence, fixity or givenness, but a contingent iterative performativity, thereby reworking this alleged conflict into an understanding of difference not as an absolute boundary between object and subject, here and there, this and that, but rather as the effects of enacted cuts *in a radical reworking of cause and effect*. (Barad 2014, pp. 173–74)

Diffraction is a material shift that changes a given compound to something new. For us, art practice, whether in online platforms or community arts workshops, highlights the diffraction of difference through understanding and communicating 'what really matters' to people and brings new dimensions into our understandings of why no 'one' human is the same. Barad's theories of entanglement demonstrate that we only exist in relation to our environments and, more than this, they allow us to see our research methods as open-ended ways of changing environments and changing people. This presents quite a particular view of the research assemblage as an entanglement and as agentive, which marks a substantive move from traditional qualitative approaches and bears alignment with what Lather and Pierre (2013) have called 'post-qualitative' research. As they so astutely note,

> entanglement makes all the categories of humanist qualitative research problematic. For example, how do we determine the 'object of our knowledge'—the 'problem' we want to study in assemblage? Can we disconnect ourselves from the mangle somehow (Self) and then carefully disconnect some other small piece of the mangle (Other) long enough to study it? What ontology has enabled us to believe the world is stable so that we can do all that individuating? And at what price? How do we think a 'research problem' in the imbrication of an agentic assemblage of diverse elements that are constantly intra-acting, never stable, never the same? (Lather and Pierre 2013, p. 630)

Gerrard et al. (2017) have written at length about what they conceive as problems with new materialism. However, for Gerrard, Rudolph and Sriprakash, whose reading of new materialism is limited, recognizing enmeshment requires relinquishing the political, whereas Barad argues that enmeshment is the political effect and affect of research methods. Removing politics is impossible. The core of the critique Gerrard et al. (2017) attempt to develop suggests that new materialist and post qualitative research cannot be political or socially useful. As we will show by drawing from our empirical research with economically disadvantaged CALD (culturally and linguistically diverse) children and communities, and our work with queer intersectional Instagram artists, new materialist and post qualitative research can be explicitly political and can respond to issues of race, class, gender and sexuality. Further, our aim in positioning feminist new materialism as being inherently political addresses the postcolonial critique that Gerrard et al. (2017) raise, suggesting that post qualitative inquiry risks operating less as new mechanisms for generative and subversive post-humanist research and more as being a process of closure and erasure. Opposing this critique, the transformative nature of feminist new materialist methodologies in which art and research converge can be seen in the work of Stacy Alaimo et al. (2008), Kester (2004), Barrett and Bolt (2014) and Nato Thompson's (2015) writing on art and activism. Thompson (2015) focuses his research on art as a political intervention and shows how art today can and does inspire innovation and dramatic transformation through activists and empowered communities. Likewise, our work brings out the politics embedded in art making and sharing, in both Instagram based communities and religious spaces. Our research creates intra-active storytelling and activism which situates the entangled diffraction of differences as a symbol of community 'togetherness'. Such an intra-active, diffractive and enmeshed methodology can be performed through a range of methods, and here we further explore two examples introduced above.

2. Methods

We bring together two different empirical projects; the first on religion, community and belonging, and the second on intersectional, queer, feminist activist art online. The first method discussed here works at the community level to examine class, race, culture, religion and identity through three rounds of three concurrent arts workshops with children (nine workshops per child), undertaken in schools, mosques, churches, service centers and housing estates, with a view to fostering and understanding interfaith relationships in childhood and understanding geographies of belonging as experienced by parents. By providing art practices as a way of communicating things children find difficult to articulate, art making can often help researchers uncover what matters most in the children's worlds and create pathways for building relationships with the children's parents. Our second method works on Instagram and examines gender identity, sexuality and community through social media activism, both via an analysis of feminist activist artists' work published online and through live Instagram interviews with the artists. We present both methods here to outline two possible examples of our broader intra-active, entangled methodology of creative research practice and use intra-action as a lens to pursue an explicitly political and politicizing research agendas.

2.1. Interfaith Childhoods: Race, Class and Community

The global landscape surrounding the mediated politics of religion and the racialization of religion changed significantly after September 11th, 2001 and the associated mediated fear of Muslim culture in 'secular' society remains a social issue in Australia and the U.K. The enduring politicization and racialization of Muslim identities that has been brought about by the post 9/11 media landscape is, in part, what we work to problematize and change through the Interfaith Childhoods project. More than this, however, the broader media framing of religion in terms of war and terror and a paucity of curriculum treating religion in Australian public schools generates a profound lack of understanding about the vernacular significance of religion in community life. Religion often sustains people and communities in adversity, and also in everyday life. This practical and significant value that can be attributed to religion is too often omitted in media reportage. Countering exactly such aggressive representations of religion, our interfaith research shows how children's creative and physical geographies can communicate quite complex information about their religions and worldviews (which include Christian, Hindu, Atheist, Muslim, Catholic). Ethnographic observations of children's faith worlds can be developed while spending consolidated time with them making art and discussing worldviews (see James 2001). Thinking through transnational and trans-local mobilities that are embodied by the children and are embedded in their representations of their religion and their own re-telling of their heritage and migration stories is a critical reflexive strategy that shows up the meaning embedded in the materiality of art making (see Hickey-Moody 2018). Children's artworks depicting identity, belonging and community offer a kind of speculative future, comprised of 'what really matters', namely, containing the social values the children hold in the highest regard. As noted, the children are from a range of religious and secular backgrounds and their imaginative futures often depict religious and secular social unity. The project, then, is designed to develop new ways of listening to community perspectives on belonging, identity and religion (Figure 1). In so doing, this research shows the intra-action of place, belief and biography, race, class and community, as central to (indeed, as co-constitutive of) children's identity.

Figure 1. Making and belonging: children and researcher share stories of home. RMIT University Human Ethics Clearance Number 21071.

The methods for this project are designed to gather three sets of data and these are:

1. Visual, imaginative data collaboratively developed with children, exploring faith, values and community
2. Focus group data from the children's parents exploring faith, values, belonging and community, which is expanded upon in detailed individual interviews with parents
3. Quantitative mappings of values, beliefs and sentiments of belonging in the communities in which the qualitative data is gathered.

The analysis below is concerned with some of the visual qualitative data from children, which offers rich depictions of the material organization of religious culture and provides multiple perspectives on experiences of faith, and shows how faith is mediated creatively across digital and popular culture. Recent images of interfaith futures developed by children from England and Australia include, but are by no means limited to, the following Figures 2–4:

Figure 2. Future city, example one from a northern English Primary School, 2018. This image features a mosque, a church and two high-density housing estates. RMIT University Human Ethics Clearance Number 21071.

Figure 3. Future city, example two from a northern English Primary School 2018. This image features a school and a hospital (the green building) a mosque, a church and a number of houses. RMIT University Human Ethics Clearance Number 21071.

Figure 4. Future city, example from an Australian church youth group, 2018. This image features a community pool, a zoo, a campfire, a large playground, a church with stained glass windows, a hospital and a number of houses. RMIT University Human Ethics Clearance Number 21071.

These three collectively devised images (Figures 2–4) are all large canvasses that have been collaboratively drawn and decorated by groups of 4–6 children aged between 4 and 9 using pastels, felt tip pens, paint pens, and collage materials (including wool, felt, cotton printed fabric). These canvasses depict imagined future cities comprised of "what really matters". Figure 2 features a mosque in the lower left-hand corner of the picture, positioned in front of a large high-rise block of flats. There is a church in the middle of the painting and further housing to the right of the canvas. At first glance, this city is clearly designed for high density living. Trees and a sun decorate the backdrop of the painting. Figure 3 features a large hospital, a mosque, a church, busy roads, houses, and a school. Strikingly, there are not a lot of people in these images, even though there are lots of places designed to be inhabited by people. Figure 4, created in Australia as opposed to the UK, bears some similarities to the UK images, although 11 people and 6 animals feature in this city, which marks a stark contrast to images from the UK, that only gesture towards people through drawings of cars.

While issues of race and class are not explicitly pictured in the works above, negotiations of issues of race and, to a lesser extent, of class, are core to the process of collaboration through which many children come to work together. More than this, negotiation of these issues is often central to these children's everyday lives. The children are from a range of predominantly non-white backgrounds and, in many instances, they are the first member of their family to have been born in the UK or Australia. With the exception of one church group, whose picture above features the swimming pools, zoo and church with stained glass, all the children in the study live and attend school in an incredibly diverse, indeed, what Steven Vertovec (2007) has called a 'superdiverse' area. Vertovec argues that superdiversity in Britain "is distinguished by a dynamic interplay of variables among an increased number of new, small and scattered, multiple-origin, transnationally connected, socio-economically differentiated and legally stratified immigrants who have arrived over the last decade" (Vertovec 2007, p. 1024). The postcode for the area in which images 2 and 3 were created is in the top 5.2% of deprived areas in the UK[2]. It is an area in Manchester, which, along with its position of economic deprivation has a substantively higher level of ethnic diversity than Manchester as a whole (UK Census 2011). It is estimated that the ward contains the third highest proportion of residents belonging to the Pakistani ethnic group[3]. The religious make up of this area is 32.7% Muslim, 30.2% Christian, 24.5% No religion, 1.2% Sikh, 1.0% Hindu, 0.9% Buddhist, 0.3% Jewish, 0.1% Agnostic[4]. As such, issues of acceptance of belief systems other than one's own are central to community life in this area.

As a result of being embedded in a superdiverse and deprived community, navigating issues of race, language, culture and religion are a required component of these children's everyday lives. Both implicitly and explicitly, these children are called to consistently respond to racialized and racializing imperatives, which can at times be advanced through social constructions of their religion. Researching with children requires the researcher to create multiple opportunities for children to communicate through indirect discourses, as often children will express themselves through doing, through the ways in which they conduct themselves and the kinds of values they perform in their expressive and representational practices. Indirect discourses are the formative materials upon which majoritarian meanings attributed to race, class and gender are built and, as such, they deserve serious attention. More than this, intervening in the configuration of discourses can be made possible through working at intersections of the discursive and non-discursive.

2.2. Thinking with Matter

The future cities depicted above, which were developed by the children, offer an opportunity for them to show how they might like to remake the world and to express the aspects of the world they find the most important. The values and desires represented in these images are shaped by the belief systems that surround the young people with whom we work with and these values shape their day to day lives as well as their imaginations. The children's visual and expressive artworks provide resources that inform our conversations with their parents, whose experiences (often these include experiences of migration) have been mediated and supported by their involvement in specific communities, often religious communities. Two further examples of children's expressive representations of their migration and / or religion stories can be found below.

Figure 5 features the blue color of the Somalian flag as the ozone layer surrounding the world, and a globe which depicts the child's journey from Somalia to the UK. The globe features a small car driving across it's midline, presumably taking the child and his family across the globe from one country to another. There is a clear sense of journey and the smallness of the car driving across the large globe gives a sense of the enormous nature of the journey that the young artist had undertaken. The boy had been living in the UK for two years, so the journey was not far from memory and is still very much part of his identity story.

---

[2] A total of 94.8% of English postcodes are less deprived than M14 7JB: (it is in the top 5.2% most deprived areas). Retrieved from: https://www.getthedata.com/postcode/M14-7JB. (GetTheData 2019)
[3] Retrieved from: Whalley Range ward profile-Manchester City Council.
[4] Retrieved from: Whalley Range Demographics (Manchester, England)-LocalStats.

Figure 5. Expressive representation of migration from Somalia to the UK drawn by a South East London boy. RMIT University Human Ethics Clearance Number 21071.

The second picture about migration, religion and identity, which is featured below, is more symbolic and less of a literal depiction of a migration story. In addition to implied geographical movements, the image addresses themes of religion and culture, family and ritual. All these themes are very important to the artist who painted the textile work.

In Figure 6, the girl who created the picture brings together family, her religion, and popular British culture through naming celebrations such as Easter and Christmas in love hearts. Looking at the image, we can get a sense of where the author/artist feels she fits in the world, especially in relation to the other people, experiences, and events that shape her. Her artwork features shades of blue that are prominent in Islamic material and visual cultures. The family tree contextualizes the child artist amongst her family and she has included heart shaped speech bubbles as balloons that express things she thinks "really matter". These include family celebrations and cultural festivals, along with the aforementioned British national holidays of Christmas and Easter, she has listed Ramadan, Eid and 'birthdays', which are grouped together in a rhizomatic clumping of the defining celebrations in this child's life.

Figure 6. Expressive representation of religion, culture and belonging. Created by a South East London girl. RMIT University Human Ethics Clearance Number 21071.

These materials (Figures 5 and 6) re-present family stories, life experiences and cultural worlds. They also offer us a different comment on the material organization of culture to the existing work of scholars who consider visual and material cultures of religion. Children position belonging in relation to both Muslim and Christian/Anglo festivals and position family clearly at the center of belonging. This perspective takes seriously the pedagogical nature of materiality, building upon Karen Barad's argument that

> Reality is therefore not a fixed essence. *Reality is an ongoing dynamic of intra-activity.* To assert that reality is made up of phenomena is not to invoke one or another form of idealism. On the contrary, phenomena are specific material configurations of the world. Phenomena are not mere human or social constructions (and they are surely not mere constructs); we don't simply make the world in our image. (Barad 2007, p. 206)

This perspective fundamentally shapes our understanding of all the subjects introduced above. Religion is not a fixed essence. Race is not a fixed essence, but it is a material agent. Religion, race, culture and society are "specific material configurations of the world" that include enmeshments of people and matter in ways that re-make meaning and attachment.

2.3. Digital, Intra-Active Methods

In our Instagram research[5], the political issues addressed predominantly relate to gender and sexuality, while race, class, reproductive rights and religion come into focus as well. Taking a feminist new materialist approach to autoethnography, our social media research creates a narrative around the subjective experiences of identity and community making in online Instagram art. With 10 international Instagram artists from various feminist political positions, we present data from our research with

---

[5] Marissa Willcox is a recipient of the RMIT RTP PhD research scholarship ID number 2266885 on which this project is funded.

Melbourne based Instagram artist Frances Cannon (@frances_cannon). We position this work and the methods discussed here, as a different method-expression of the same new materialist methodology performed in the Interfaith Childhoods' project. The methods demonstrate the politics embedded in art making and sharing processes, as the themes discussed in both the Interfaith Childhoods art workshops and in the Instagram research draw a transversal line joining race, religion, belonging, gender, sexuality, identity and more. What stays constant is the underlying philosophical commitment to enmeshment and to intra-active methods that show us how various differences are diffracted through art to create this 'togetherness'. Performing an Instagram live interview on the participants' Instagram page creates an intra-action of bodies (Figure 7). We blur the imaginary and real barriers that divide the digital and social worlds through this process (Hillis et al. 2015). By embodying the experience of being and performing live on Instagram, we are given a share of the participants' world and online community, and in effect, aim to minimize the much-contested qualitative researcher/subject power imbalance (Dolphijn and van der Tuin 2012). Instagram live interviews are framed here as a new materialist way of rethinking subjective experiences of identity and community making. The interview questions are tailored to fit the individual activist themes, and they change based on the participants thoughts/topics of interest during the live engagement. The conversation is broadcasted through their Instagram live story immediately, which contributes to their goal of community building through social media engagement and digital communication.

Figure 7. Intra-acting the interview. RMIT University Human Ethics Clearance Number 21229.

A live intra-active interview thus, is co-created with the participant in a way which privileges the *being* over *knowing* in researcher/participant relationships (Back 2012; Lather and Pierre 2013). We demonstrate how bodies and things are not separate, and show their inter-relationship is vital to how we come to know ourselves as humans and interact with our environments. All research participants are feminist, and most are queer-identified. Most are also same-sex attracted. Participants' art practice and their arts-based community become a site for research, and a conversational tool. The topics that participants discuss in their interviews draw them back to the themes found in the participants' art online. This entanglement is discussed in front of the participant's live audience: their followers and community.

> Situated knowledges is not merely about knowing/seeing from somewhere (as in having a perspective), but about taking account of how the specific prosthetic embodiment of the technologically enhanced visualising apparatus matters to practices of knowing. (Barad 2008, p. 326, quoting Haraway 1997)

To put Haraway's point another way, having and gaining knowledge is therefore not a practice of seeing or reflecting from a removed position, seeing co-creates the position, it is a process that is concerned with embodying and being with/in the place of inquiry. As affective researchers, understanding only comes through *doing, being, making,* and *feeling*. Especially in interviews, "those involved in the interview come together to form an assemblage that exceeds the individuals themselves" (Willink and Shukri 2018, p. 188). Non-hegemonic gender and sexual identities and themes of online community inclusion become enmeshed with aesthetics of style through conversations with artists that explore these themes in their artwork. The method is outlined in greater detail below.

Frances Cannon's art takes on a feminist activist perspective while also illustrating pieces of her life and aspects of her own identity. Figure 8 is a reflection of the experience of being a woman on Instagram and brings up the notion that traditionally, representation of women's bodies in the media has been (and still is) 'for the male gaze'. This post (Figure 8) now has over 8000 likes and more than 100 comments. Frances initiates a dialogue around feminism, body positivity, the media, and unsafe online spaces through this transgressive art. Frances Cannon's followers are seen coming together to discuss their different experiences relating to this image in the comments section, and her art looks to unite them in their varying feminist political agendas.

Figure 8. "I AM NOT A PIECE OF MEAT!" from @frances_cannon, Instagram, March 2019. RMIT University Human Ethics Clearance Number 21229.

Coming from a new materialist lens and working with intra-action rather than interaction, we build on Dolphijn and van der Tuin's (2012) approach to understanding interviews as outlined in *New Materialism: Interviews and Cartographies*. They describe how the attitude towards interviews should be seen as an intra-action, stating:

> Qualitatively shifting any atomist metaphysics, intra-action conceptualizes that it is the action *between* (and not *in*-between) that matters. In other words, it is not the interviewers or

the interviewee or even the oeuvre of the interviewee that deserves our special attention, but it is the sense of orientation that the interview gave rise to (the action itself) that should engender us. For it is in the action itself that new materialism announces itself. (Dolphijn and van der Tuin 2012, Introduction)

This approach conceives the interview process as an ongoing intra-action of bodies and places. The objective of the researcher in any new materialist methodology is to *become with* and be *entangled* in the research as it progresses. Engaging with "complexity, uncertainty and risk" as Jen Ross (2017) suggests in digital media-based pedagogy, we embrace continuous "not yet-ness" in methodological processes. Through online live interviewing, 'data' is made instantly available to the participant's global community of followers and the live nature of the interview makes every discussion unique. Planned topics for discussion can often change in response to the participant's political agenda and online persona. This intra-action is a way of making space for social change by initiating academic interest in the intersectional dialogues of inclusion that are being broadcast online, therefore encouraging and supporting communities that diffract differences.

2.4. Creating and Mediating the Feminist Self: Live Broadcasts

We outline the live Instagram method here, alongside an initial ethnographic observation that encapsulates the experience of entering Frances Cannon's community space, as the community surrounding Cannon's artwork is a powerful agent in supporting her work: "the virtual, therefore, can be understood as the potentialities, investments, and imaginations concerning the present and the possible shape of things to come" (Hillis et al. 2015, p. 9). The fieldnote excerpt below expresses the feelings of community and belonging that exist amongst the feminists in this digital space. Without meeting Frances Cannon's followers in person, entering her studio and entering her Instagram story show the levels of complexity in modern identities of community, time and space. We think through how these online and offline spaces for inclusion and acceptance diffract feelings of difference.

The method for this project situates the researcher in an ongoing intra-active engagement online while blurring the distinctions between the online/offline experience. Three different methods are enacted to build a feminist autoethnographic narrative based on case studies using 10 international Instagram artists:

1. An initial private semi-structured interview, exploring how feminist artists represent and express gender, sexuality, feminism and the body in art practice on Instagram.
2. A follow up interview, conducted on the participants' Instagram live that engages in a discussion around gender, feminism, sexuality and the body but with a lens to understanding the feminist activist art community and mapping the artists' engagement within that community (this is visually recorded through the engagement of their followers with the live video).
3. A continued and ongoing documentation of the artists' engagement within this global community by following their stories and posts and actively participating in this space. This is recorded through screenshots and recording the liking, commenting, and sharing of the artist's work across their various pages and stories to map community responses and sentiment.

2.5. Ethnographic Observation: Frances Cannon's Studio, 19 February 2019

I walked into the wrong room. Frances Cannon had invited me to her Coburg studio to conduct our second interview on Instagram live. The building had two floors. While I stood in the dark studio gallery on the bottom floor with walls covered in art depicting naked women, kissing women, breasts, blood, and the color blue, the room seemed to envelop me. I was in her space. There were other artist's paintings and drawings for sale on the walls, all with a feminist theme. I announced myself, but no one seemed to hear. I left the unlit gallery and stood outside in the hot summer air again. On the sprawling Coburg square, plots of the same brown grass stretched before me, the soil underneath them drying even more in the Australian summer heat. The 1990s style, single story, brick bungalows shimmered, still, as the trains blew past. Frances opened the side door to the building and waved me in. She kissed me on the cheek and showed me upstairs to a somewhat less intimate room, filled with desks and art and paper everywhere. It was an artist's haven. I quickly used the bathroom before our interview and noticed piled old art canvases on the floor, discarded (Figure 9). The counter was dusty and the air smelled of dry paint. I came out, and saw she was settled in her corner getting her iPhone tripod set up. I had the same one. Frances flowed around her desk to clear her art supplies away. Her denim dress swung as she cleared paper and canvases to the floor, she spoke about her upcoming solo art show. I said I would go. We got ready for our Instagram live interview and talked about the people that would comment, the questions and topics we might discuss. A friend of hers sat in the background, silently painting. As we turned on the live video on her Instagram story, I introduced myself to her audience of followers and prompted questions around gender, sexuality, the body and feminism, all relating to her art. Her Instagram community followed suit. The comments section on our live interview was flowing with likes and statements of support, awareness, inclusion, acceptance. When Frances spoke about her queerness others jumped in with heart emojis and signs and symbols of love. She had hundreds of people commenting as we spoke, and our conversation carried on. It felt rude not to stop the whole thing and address them, her followers. It was like we were speaking to them, for them. But we continued on with the interview. Sitting oddly close together yet looking forward at a tiny black phone screen. We were both sweating, shimmering like the brown bungalow houses lining the street outside. I was so nervous to be on a live platform, performing for her followers. What if I 'messed up'? What if I said the 'wrong thing'? We both smiled when the 'Feminists from Brazil' Instagram account commented on our chat with a 'we can do it' strong arm emoji and expressed their support for our conversation topics. Other followers from her community expressed their love for Frances's art and style. When I asked her about her artistic style in relation to her personal background, Frances said that she grew up in quite a conservative Christian household where queerness wasn't talked about. I then realized what all of her followers were doing online watching this video. It was the same thing Frances was doing by creating her art, just looking for a place and people to connect to, to feel loved and accepted, a place to belong. Instagram artists have created that space, an online community of belonging and acceptance.

Figure 9. Discarded. Canvases on the floor in Frances's Studio. RMIT University Human Ethics Clearance Number 21229.

There was little to say when I left this online interview space, I felt like I had entered into a new world, a world of inclusion, acceptance and togetherness where feminism was at the forefront of everyone's minds and sexuality was a celebrated topic of discussion. We ended the Instagram live interview with advice for the future, and Frances encouraged her followers to love themselves, their whole selves. Digital heart emojis had flown across the screen for the whole 30 minutes. I packed up, hugged her and left. I stepped back into the street and noticed the square plots again, so brown, so alike, yet at the same time, still so different.

2.6. Mixing with Matter

Willcox's ethnographic fieldnotes from Frances Cannon's interview show the fluidity of entering into her global Instagram community while sitting (sweating) in her Coburg studio. The element of *being* and *performing* in the interview as a live action is taken as data and a mode of embodied engagement. By doing a live interview, the conversation about sexuality and body positivity is immediately translated to Frances's 186K followers. The interview becomes a political and feminist statement to a live, attentive audience. Coming from the feminist new materialist frame of interviewing and understanding feminist identities in the contexts with which they are made (Colman 2014; McTague et al. 2017), we apply this concept to the new materialist trope that "every actual object is surrounded by a cloud of virtuality" (Hillis et al. 2015, p. 9). This virtuality can be seen here in the intra-active engagements between layers of love heart emojis, black phone screens, sweating bodies, followers' comments, a flowing dress, and conversations about art. When taken together, these intra-actions initiate a blurring of the boundaries between communities and identities as we see them being made. In this live discussion of Frances's politics and activist art, we can feel the diffraction of differences enabled through this digital platform as she opens up an online space for a dialogue, inclusion and acceptance (Figure 10).

Figure 10. Digital Diffraction. RMIT University Human Ethics Clearance Number 21229.

By adopting the political position that Instagram can sometimes play a role in reproducing and reinforcing traditional gender norms and heterosexual representations (Caldeira et al. 2018, p. 23) and by intra-acting the interview in a live setting, the research aim becomes to actively change heteronormative, patriarchal online narratives. This method is built to amplify the experiences and identities of feminists, fat women, queer women, WOC, trans women, and non-binary artists whom often feel left out of the heteronormative online narrative, by positioning them at the centre of their identity and community making in the research process (Crenshaw 1989). It brings people of different backgrounds and experiences together over their respect for art and intersectionality, through the digital interface of Instagram. Rather than use traditional focus groups or interviews, this live style of interviewing with an aesthetic, digital, focus, offers qualitative researchers a chance to bring non-traditional representations of gender and sexuality into global online communities who share aligned interests. It serves an activist agenda by contributing a live discussion to the feminist movement online that fights for gender equality, queer inclusion and the representation of more non-white, fat, disabled and queer bodies in media spaces (Afful and Ricciardelli 2015; Robinson et al. 2019). By researching the users of these online social spaces with the same methods they use to navigate their own identities and communities, this methodology of Instagram live interviewing creates space to amplify the experiences of those who feel underrepresented in the online heteronormative narrative.

3. Conclusions

In both sets of the above methods, our methodology of diffractive, intra-active and entangled making with community is explored creatively. We present community focused, intra-active, arts-based research strategies for interrogating and understanding online expressions of community and belonging. With our theoretical frame inspired by entanglement, diffraction and intra-action in new materialist methodologies, we identify the fact that creative methods are a way of knowing about communities by *being with* communities in playful, fun and non-intrusive ways. Here, we agree with Rebecca Coleman, who states:

> Drawing attention to a collective or individual sense of enjoyment may seem insignificant, but I think it's interesting for a number of reasons. For one thing, there's something to say about social science methodologies being fun and playful. This is perhaps especially important in the context of what Roger Burrows and Mike Savage (2007) call the 'coming crisis of empirical sociology', where they note that methods initially developed by sociology and wider social sciences (such as interviews, and surveys) are increasingly employed in commercial sectors—meaning both that the methodological expertise by which sociology has traditionally defined itself no longer belong to it alone, and that new audiences and markets are being enrolled in what are sometimes more agile and fun versions of these methods. So, the question of how social sciences might re-develop their own methods that are themselves fun is crucial. There is then a politics and ethics to how this question might be addressed. (Coleman 2016, online)

Our methods have to move with the times if they are to remain useful. As we argued earlier, the virtual and social worlds shown as sites for research are both understood in terms of how the potentialities and imaginaries co-constitute each other and, in turn, are responsible for the other. Each community not only diffracts their differences through art, but intra-acts with the other through an on-going time space that is concerned with the ethics of understanding and ultimately with becoming *enmeshed* as a community.

We have also discussed how our methodologies embody theories from the posthuman era, by doing research that thinks *with* the body. Rosi Braidotti (2013) outlines posthumanism in her book *The Posthuman* by demonstrating what it means to think *within* and *through* the body. She presents a particular kind of knowledge around difference as relating back to early humanism:

> This Eurocentric paradigm [of 'Humanism'] implies the dialectics of self and other, and the binary logic of identity and otherness as respectively the motor for and the cultural logic of universal Humanism. Central to this universalistic posture and its binary logic is the notion of 'difference' as pejoration. Subjectivity is equated with consciousness, universal rationality, and

self-regulating ethical behaviour, whereas Otherness is defined as its negative and specular counterpart. In so far as difference spells inferiority, it acquires both essentialist and lethal connotations for people who get branded as 'others'. These are the sexualized, racialized, and naturalized others, who are reduced to the less than human status of disposable bodies. We are all humans, but some of us are just more mortal than others. (Braidotti 2013, p. 3)

Braidotti's advancement of feminist post humanism and feminist new materialism are research practices that constitute a field in which we situate our research; a field which is (as the above quote demonstrates) explicitly politicized and politicizing. As we intra-act within art-based spaces, feminist activists and children express their feelings of cultural belonging, acceptance, difference, disagreement and togetherness through colour, texture, making, and doing. In community arts workshops and on Instagram, we intervene in the dissemination and re-production of problematic aspects of racializing and gendering discourses. By both intra-acting in live interviews and intra-acting in arts workshops, we learn and feel and change with the people with whom we work, as opposed to measuring and quantifying their being. We initiate a diffraction of differences in our approaches, by not privileging the *knowing* in research, but privileging the *being with*. In understanding *being with* as an intra-active, entangled, contextually specific experience, we aim to make new ways for people to come together and share their knowledges, experiences, and differences which help them to feel they belong or provide resources with which to negotiate difference. Understanding the collaborative production of feelings reminds us that all feelings and identities are intra-active, entangled products of communities, which we conceive as collections of difference.

Author Contributions: The authors worked on this project in conjunction with eachother forming theoretical discussions through their shared methods and methodological frames. A.H.-M. provided the first draft while M.W. expanded on the initial writing. They finalized the finished draft together.

Funding: Professor Hickey-Moody is a recipient of The Australian Research Council Future Fellowship project number FT 160100293 'Early Start Arts to Counter Radicalization' on which this project is funded. Marissa Willcox is a recipient of the RMIT RTP PhD research scholarship ID number 2266885 on which this project is funded.

Conflicts of Interest: The authors declare no conflict of interest.

References

Afful, Adwoa A., and Rose Ricciardelli. 2015. Shaping the online fat acceptance movement: Talking about body image and beauty standards. *Journal of Gender Studies* 24: 453–72. [CrossRef]

Alaimo, Stacy, Susan Hekman, and Susan J. Hekman. 2008. *Material Feminisms*. Bloomington: Indiana University Press.

Back, Les. 2012. Live sociology: Social research and its futures. *The Sociological Review* 60: 18–39. [CrossRef]

Barad, Karen. 2003. Posthumanist Performativity: Toward an Understanding of How Matter Comes to Matter. *Signs* 28: 801–31. [CrossRef]

Barad, Karen. 2007. *Meeting the Universe Halfway: Quantum Physics and the Entanglement of Matter and Meaning*; Durham: Duke University Press. Available online: https://www.dukeupress.edu/Meeting-the-Universe-Halfway/ (accessed on 10 June 2019).

Barad, Karen. 2008. Queer Causation and the Ethics of Mattering. In *Queering the Non/Human*. Edited by Noreen Giffney and Myra J. Hird. Hampshire and Burlington: Ashgate Publishing, Ltd., pp. 311–38.

Barad, Karen. 2014. Diffracting Diffraction: Cutting Together-Apart. *Parallax* 20: 168–87. [CrossRef]

Barrett, Estelle, and Barbara Bolt, eds. 2014. *Material Inventions: Applying Creative Arts Research*. London: I.B. Tauris.

Braidotti, Rosi. 2013. *The Posthuman*; Cambridge and Maldern: Polity Press. Available online: http://ebookcentral.proquest.com (accessed on 10 June 2019).

Caldeira, Sofia P., Sander De Ridder, and Sofie Van Bauwel. 2018. Exploring the Politics of Gender Representation on Instagram: Self-representations of Feminity. *Journal of Diversity and Gender Studies* 5: 23–42. [CrossRef]

Coleman, Rebecca. 2016. Collaging workshops II: Play and Uncertainty. [Temporalrepertoires]. Available online: http://www.temporalrepertoires.org/blog/collaging-workshops-ii-play-and-uncertainty (accessed on 12 July 2019).

Colman, Felicity. 2014. Digital feminicity: Predication and measurement, materialist informatics and images. *Artnodes*. [CrossRef]

Crenshaw, Kimberle. 1989. Demarginalizing the Intersection of Race and Sex: A Black Feminist Critique of Antidiscrimination Doctrine, Feminist Theory and Antiracist Politics. *University of Chicago Legal Forum* 1: 139. Available online: https://chicagounbound.uchicago.edu/uclf/vol1989/iss1/8 (accessed on 24 June 2019).

Deleuze, Gilles, and Félix Guattari. 1994. *What Is Philosophy?* New York and Chichester: Columbia University Press.

Dolphijn, Rick, and Iris van der Tuin. 2012. *New Materialism: Interviews & Cartographies*. London: Open Humanities Press. [CrossRef]

Gerrard, Jessica, Sophie Rudolph, and Arathi Sriprakash. 2017. The Politics of Post-Qualitative Inquiry: History and Power. *Qualitative Inquiry* 23: 384–94. [CrossRef]

GetTheData. 2019. M14 7JB Maps, Stats, and Open Data. Available online: https://www.getthedata.com/postcode/M14-7JB (accessed on 1 July 2019).

Haraway, Donna J. 1997. ModestWitness@SecondMillennium.FemaleMan©-Meets_OncoMouse ™: Feminism and Technoscience. *Journal of the History of Biology* 30: 494–97.

Hickey-Moody, Anna. 2017. Arts Practice as Method, Urban Spaces and Intra-Active Faiths. *International Journal of Inclusive Education* 21: 1083–96. [CrossRef]

Hickey-Moody, Anna. 2018. New Materialism, Ethnography, and Socially Engaged Practice: Space-Time Folds and the Agency of Matter. *Qualitative Inquiry*. [CrossRef]

Hickey-Moody, Anna. 2019. Ways of Knowing Failure' *MAI: Feminism and Visual Culture*. MAI. May 15. Available online: https://maifeminism.com/three-ways-of-knowing-failure/ (accessed on 22 June 2019).

Hickey-Moody, Anna, and Mia Harrison. 2018. Socially Engaged Art and Affective Pedagogy: A Study in Inter-Faith Understanding. *Tate Papers* No. 29. Available online: https://www.tate.org.uk/research/publications/tate-papers/29/socially-engaged-art-and-affective-pedagogy (accessed on 24 July 2019).

Hickey-Moody, Anna, and Marissa Willcox. 2019. Material Expressions of Religious Culture. In *Religion, Hypermobility and Digital Media in Global Asia: Faith, Flows and Fellowship*. Amsterdam: Amsterdam University Press, Forthcoming.

Hillis, Ken, Susanna Paasonen, and Michael Petit, eds. 2015. *Networked Affect*. Massachusetts: MIT Press.

James, Allison. 2001. Ethnography in the Study of Children and Childhood. In *Handbook of Ethnography*. Edited by Paul Atkinson, Amanda Coffey, Sara Delamont, John Lofland and Lyn Lofland. London: Routledge, pp. 246–57.

Kester, Grant H. 2004. *Conversation Pieces: Community and Communication in Modern Art*. Berkeley: University of California Press.

Lather, Patti, and Elizabeth A. St. Pierre. 2013. Post-Qualitative Research. *International Journal of Qualitative Studies in Education* 26: 629–33. [CrossRef]

McTague, Tricia, Carissa Froyum, and Barbara J. Risman. 2017. Learning about inequality from kids: Interviewing strategies for getting beneath equality rhetoric. *Researching Children and Youth: Methodological Issues, Strategies, and Innovations* 22: 277–301.

Palmer, Helen. 2016. *Deleuze and Futurism: A Manifesto for Nonsense*. London: Bloomsbury.

Ringrose, Jessica, and Emma Renold. 2016. Cows, Cabins and Tweets: Posthuman Intra-active Affect and Feminist Fire in Secondary School. In *Posthuman Research Practices in Education*. Edited by Carol Taylor and Christina Hughes. Abingdon: Taylor & Francis Group, pp. 220–41. [CrossRef]

2019. *The Art of Feminism: Images that Shaped the Fight for Equality*; San Francisco: Chronicle Books. Available online: https://shop.tate.org.uk/the-art-of-feminism-images-that-shaped-the-fight-for-equality/22015.html (accessed on 19 July 2019).

Ross, Jen. 2017. Speculative method in digital education research. *Learning, Media and Technology* 42: 214–29. [CrossRef]

Thompson, Nato. 2015. *Seeing Power: Art and Activism in the 21st Century*. Brooklyn: Melville House Publishing.

van der Tuin, Iris. 2008. Third Wave Materialism: New Feminist Epistemologies and the Generation of European Women's Studies. Ph.D. thesis, Utrecht University, Utrecht, The Netherlands.

van der Tuin, Iris. 2015. *Generational Feminism: A New Materialist Introduction to a Generative Approach*. London: Rowman and Littlefield.

UK Census. 2011. QPZM Local Stats. Available online: http://whalley-range.localstats.co.uk/census-demographics/england/north-west/manchester/whalley-range (accessed on 20 July 2019).

Vertovec, Steven. 2007. Super-diversity and its implications. *Ethnic and Racial Studies* 30: 1024–54. [CrossRef]

Willink, Kate G., and Salma T. Shukri. 2018. Performative interviewing: Affective attunement and reflective affective analysis in interviewing. *Text and Performance Quarterly* 38: 187–207. [CrossRef]

© 2019 by the authors. Licensee MDPI, Basel, Switzerland. This article is an open access article distributed under the terms and conditions of the Creative Commons Attribution (CC BY) license (http://creativecommons.org/licenses/by/4.0/).

Article

Moving with Touch: Entanglements of a Child, Valentine's Day Cards, and Research–Activism against Sexual Harassment in Pre-Teen Peer Cultures

Suvi Pihkala *, Tuija Huuki and Vappu Sunnari

Faculty of Education, University of Oulu, FI-90014 Oulu, Finland
* Correspondence: suvi.pihkala@oulu.fi

Received: 17 May 2019; Accepted: 22 July 2019; Published: 26 July 2019

Abstract: In this paper, we respond to feminist new materialist scholars' calls to explore what research in the field of gendered and sexual violence can be, do, and become. This paper explores the microprocesses of change within the more-than-human child–card entanglements as part of our research–activist campaign addressing sexual harassment in pre-teen peer cultures. Drawing on one of our creative workshops, we generate three analytical readings that map touch. We focus, first, on the intra-action of bodies, objects, and abstractions that reconfigures painful experiences of harassment for recognition; second, on the affective charge in moments and movements of response and resistance; and third, on what else touch can become when it travels across time–space domains as part of our research–activism. Re-engaging with our research–activism, we propose that different kinds of touch converge into a sensing-feeling, inherently ethico-political, matter-realizing apparatus that reconfigures painful experiences of gendered and sexual harassment for recognition, response, and resistance. Connecting to feminist new materialist endeavors to envision and enact response-able research, we propose that 'moving with touch' helps us shed light on the microprocesses of change in generative ways—that is, in ways that recraft response-abilities and invite movement.

Keywords: Barad; children; creative methods; feminist new materialisms; research–activism; response-ability; sexual harassment; touch

1. Introduction

Sexual harassment was brought to renewed attention in 2017, prompted by the global '#MeToo' movement. Having spent nearly 20 years exploring gender and sexual power plays among children in school settings, our research team—including Tuija, who was following the debate closely—was deeply affected by the discussion, which mostly ignored the ways sexual harassment connects to and permeates children's peer cultures. This combination of the 'hashtag feminism' (Mendes et al. 2018) against sexual harassment, the public debate, and our numerous research encounters with children marked the 'beginning in the middle' of our research–activist project. Theoretically, our research–activist approach was inspired by feminist new materialist and, in particular, 'phEmaterialist' work (e.g., Renold and Ringrose 2019), which have generatively merged feminist research with Deleuzian/Spinozian activist philosophies (e.g., Braidotti 2013) and the theories of micropolitics of change (Manning 2016; Massumi 2015) and affect (e.g., Blackman and Venn 2010) in order to envision ways of doing educational research capable of generating material changes in wider social spheres (e.g., Renold 2018; Ringrose et al. 2019).

The creative arts-based research-activist project, titled #MeToo Postscriptum, that shaped the direction of this article, was designed and implemented by two of the authors—Tuija and Suvi—during the weeks before Valentine's Day in 2018. It emerged from Tuija's broader ongoing research and from a long continuum of research on gendered and sexual force relations by the authors (Huuki and Renold 2016; Huuki et al. 2010; Holford et al. 2013; Pihkala and Huuki 2019; Sunnari et al. 2002; Sunnari 2010).

Although it is often discussed only in relation to adults, research shows that sexual harassment—verbal, physical, material, emotional, or psychological sexual abuses of power—also affect young people in multiple, contradictory manners as normalized, everyday hetero-sexisms circulating within young peer cultures, media, and the wider social and cultural discourses (Gillander Gådin 2012; Holford et al. 2013; Meyer 2009; Renold 2013; Stein 2007; Sunnari 2010; Sunnari et al. 2002). However, young people are left with insufficient support for navigating these often contentious terrains of gender and sexuality (Renold 2013). Drawing inspiration from child-led activism in Wales (Renold 2018, 2019; Renold and Ringrose 2019), the #MeToo Postscriptum campaign engaged children aged 10–12 years in creative workshops to explore their experiences of sexual harassment and to communicate those experiences to decisionmakers and the public.

In this paper, we return to and re-engage with one of the workshops, a workshop with a group of eight girls,[1] and map the iterative intra-action of Valentine's Day cards, girls, experiences of past harassment, the research–activist campaign, and our own engagements and entanglements during the campaign. In re-engaging with the workshop, we employ touch as a steering concept that reanimates and enlivens within and through three analytically enacted moments at focus in this paper. Drawing on Barad's (2007) agential realism, with the first moment, we map more-than-human touch, focusing on the materiality of the workshop. We render visible how bodies, tables, movement, space, objects, postscripts, past, present, and research–activism intra-act, generating conditions of possibility for painful experiences to reconfigure for recognition. Then, we map what else touch can do, focusing on the affective charge in the moments and movements of response and resistance in the intra-action of past experiences, Valentine's cards, and a makeshift mailbox. Our third and final analysis maps what else touch can become as it gathers up and holds together across time–space domains, reaching towards, sticking to us, and traveling to wider change-making terrains. Mapping and moving with touch enable us to become open to the microprocesses and micropolitics of change and, as explored in this paper, to the ways in which painful experiences of harassment can be reconfigured for recognition, response, and resistance.

As invested and interested in co-constructing and theorizing response-able, everyday practices of change-making (Huuki 2019; Pihkala et al. 2018; Pihkala 2018), this paper contributes to the recent calls to envision response-able research and practice and to illuminate and theorize the microprocesses of change in our research endeavors (Ringrose et al. 2019; Renold 2018). 'Moving with touch' within our creative research–activism sheds light on the affordances of feminist new materialism-inspired approaches that are attuned to materiality, relationality, and becoming. We argue that our research–activism, predicated on creative, multimodal, more-than-human sense abilities, fostered conditions in which unwanted, painful, silenced, and unaddressed experiences could be reconfigured for recognition, response, and resistance in ways that exceed the limits of humanistic and talk-based modes of engagement. Beginning from within entanglements and relationality, as opposed to pre-existing subjects and objects, enables us to attend to the material-discursive practices of body, object, gesture, movement, silence, voice, space, history, feeling, and touch and how these human and more-than-human elements intra-act, producing particular and contingent outcomes (Barad 2007). We maintain that working from within such entanglements enables elbow room for the unexpected and

---

[1] Informed by our long-term work with children around sensitive topics of gender and sexual harassment, the workshops were held in single-sex groups with the aim of ensuring safe possibilities for the participants to explore and communicate their experiences of their friendship and relationship cultures. Within the scope of this research, it was not possible to address the children's experiences of gender, but grounded in our long-term research on gender and power in child peer cultures, we were familiar with the specific context of our research–activism in Finland. In this context, issues of gender are sensitive, unaddressed, and often silenced, which make them difficult to address. The grouping by assumed gender aligned with the accustomed and dominant practices of the schools. It was based on our previous experiences of working in mixed-gender groups where the sensitivity and difficulty of the topic causes anxiety and dominant modes of gender expression become enforced. In order to work with and rework gender dichotomies, the groups were thus divided by assumed gender. However, our approach during our engagements with the children remained sensitive to the children's diverse gender expressions.

emergent and prompts us to not limit our inquiry to interpretations and instead invest in how research can be made to matter in the world (Ringrose et al. 2019). By thinking with theory and moving with touch, we make a speculative gesture towards theorizing what else touch can be, do, and become. Methodologically, mapping different kinds of touches causes them to converge into a sensing-feeling, inherently ethico-political, matter-realizing apparatus that yields a nuanced account of the intra-active moments when subtle shifts of change occur. It does so in generative ways—that is, in ways that recraft response-abilities and incite and invite movement.

2. Each Intra-Action Matters: Envisioning the Microprocesses of Change in Research against Sexual Harassment in Pre-Teen Peer Cultures

This paper connects to the expansive work inspired by feminist new materialist theories related to affect, materiality, and the relationality of human and more-than-human others (e.g., Barad 2007; Braidotti 2013; Dolphijn and van der Tuin 2012). This work has elicited heightened attunement and thoughtfulness in feminist research and social sciences more widely with respect to how bodies, objects, and discourses affect one another and are affected upon and how power, agency, and change, for example, are imagined (Fox and Alldred 2016; Ringrose et al. 2019). In phEmaterialist work, the reimagination of how gender, power, and sexuality matter in children's lives and, importantly, how change and transformation could be evoked (Renold and Ringrose 2019), has prompted—to use a term borrowed from Barad (2007) and Haraway (2008)—response-able research and pedagogy (Renold 2018; Ringrose et al. 2019; Taylor 2018). This call also acts as our motivation and inspiration to move with touch as we work to attune to and capture the subtle shifts of change within our research–activism.

In gauging such 'microprocesses of change' as they occur, we employ three pivotal threads from Barad's ethico-onto-epistemology. Barad (2007) introduced the idea of agential realism, proposing that the world and things 'come to matter' through agential cuts enacted through ongoing intra-action; that is, objects, abstractions, discourses, and even space and time do not pre-exist their relatings. This means that phenomena, such as gender and sexual harassment as the object of our inquiry and activism, too, must be understood to become intelligible through specific and contingent material-discursive arrangements or apparatuses of bodily production (Barad 2007). It is perhaps particularly in the matterings of gender and sexuality—and sexual harassment—where Barad's thinking works to make visible the agential force of discursive practices upon matter, and vice versa.

In this paper, intra-action, then, heightens our attention in relation to the dynamic ontological entanglements of human and more-than-human others—that is, how bodies, objects, movement, time, discourse, feelings, and gestures intra-act within and through the workshop. Furthermore, for Barad (2007), time does not work in a mode of linearity. This challenges the ways we understand change, which can no longer be perceived to follow from a past that once was but, rather, emerges through the iterative differentiating and reworking of a past that was never left behind and a future that is already present (Barad 2007). In this sense, each intra-action matters as a more-than-human and more-than-present encounter that holds the possibility 'to breathe life into ever new possibilities for living justly' (Barad 2007, p. x).

Considering the past experiences of pain, hurt, silence, and denial materializing for recognition through our research–activist apparatus against sexual harassment, Barad's thinking helps us attune to the intra-active entanglements anew. It helps us consider how, as we move, craft, and talk with the children, the intra-active entanglements of bodies, things, moments, and places come together and hold the possibility for making a difference in how sexual harassment matters. There is a breathtaking intimacy to this, as Barad (2014) writes. She brings the ethico-onto-epistemology of agential realism in touch with touch, stating that 'touching, sensing, is what matter does, or rather, what matter is: matter is condensations of response-ability' (Barad 2014, p. 161, italics removed). Indeed, the ethicality at the marrow of mattering—as captured in the hyphenated notion of 'response-ability' (Barad 2007; Haraway 2008)—is 'always already integral to the world's ongoing intra-active becoming and not-becoming'

(Barad 2010, p. 265). It is an invitation and an obligation to enable and welcome the response of the other that inhabits 'each meeting' (Barad 2007).

Enriching our thinking about the intra-active entanglements of our research–activist encounters with touch and response-ability enables us to imagine the intra-activity at stake as materially crowded, affectively charged, and temporally rich—more-than-human and more-than-present—entanglements that are ethical from the get go. This thinking also reanimates 'our responsibility to be in touch' (Barad 2014) in our research–activist endeavors. As we maintain, how we co-compose the materials, creative practices, and human and more-than-human others matters. It matters to the ways we can help children identify and share with others their experiences and concerns related to sexual harassment and how we can foster possibilities for change in children's peer cultures. Indeed, Barad (2007, p. 89) asks us to 'tak[e] responsibility for the fact that our practices matter; the world is materialized differently through different practices'. This ethics as 'always-already'—response-ability (Barad 2007; Haraway 2008)—casts a challenge and obligation to 'cultivate the capacity to respond' (Haraway 2016, p. 7) and to reimagine the ethico-political potentiality in 'each meeting' in our attempt to both make inquiries into and co-compose conditions for co-flourishing.

3. Method and Materials: Moving with Touch

As part of the #MeToo Postscriptum campaign, we organized and implemented 17 arts-based workshop sessions focusing on gendered and sexual harassment in pre-teen peer relations with a total of 150 children aged 10–12 years at schools in Finland. When organizing the workshops, we endeavored to create specific conditions that provide access to new ground and enable safe and creative intra-action (Barad 2007), so as to allow the participants to explore the ambivalences, contradictions, pains, and pleasures embedded in the gendered and sexual power relations of pre-teen peer cultures. Such conditions could be understood to constitute what Massumi (2015) calls 'enabling constraints', which propose a specific object of concern without, however, imposing preconceived notions about the final destination or outcome (Massumi 2015, p. 73). Enabling constraints, as we built upon them here, are carefully and purposefully made arrangements that cultivate conditions of response (Barad 2007; Haraway 2008) and that simultaneously mark our response-ability and accountability with respect to the becomings and not-becomings we help enact (Barad 2007).

The workshops involved activities related to the topic of sexual harassment. During the workshops, the children engaged in discussions and exploration of gendered and sexualized peer cultures and sexual harassment, created and drew Valentine's Day cards, and—if they chose to do so—wrote their own experiences of harassment in the postscripts of their cards.[2] In addition to the workshops with the children, a pop-up stand was set up in a university café to allow student teachers and faculty members to partake the campaign by sharing their own childhood experiences of harassment. Through our research–activism, our aims were to generate data on children's experiences of sexual harassment in peer relations,[3] communicate those experiences with children to wider audiences, and engage in political debate and social transformation. As part of the latter, after the workshops, the research team collected and sent the cards to every member of the Finnish Parliament and published excerpts from the notes and cards on the campaign website (Huuki and Pihkala 2018). The cards with the postscripts were intended to remind decisionmakers and the Finnish public of the need for systematic and consistent work to address sexual harassment, which affects not only adults but also children.

---

[2] Occurring in advance of Valentine's Day, in our project, the #MeToo became linked with the postscript section of a Valentine's Day card. The postscript worked to make visible the often-ignored nature and the silence regarding sexual harassment in pre-teen peer relations (Pihkala and Huuki 2019). Using the hashtag connected the project to the momentum afforded by the digital feminist activism of the #MeToo movement (Mendes et al. 2018).

[3] As part of our wider interest in investigating gender and sexual harassment in pre-teen peer cultures, the workshops were video-recorded, accumulating a total of 27 h of audio–visual recordings, 108 pages of transcripts, 15 pages of extended field notes, and 210 digitalized cards, of which the data for this paper involve 2 h and 36 min of audio–visual recordings from the workshop session in question.

The human and more-than-human 'participants' of the campaign, such as the children, researchers, public, the decisionmakers, hands, chairs, tables, space, paper slips, pens, and arts and crafts; and the multiple modalities of the creative activities, such as the movement, crafting, speech, and writing, were understood as active and lively coplayers that came together in unexpected ways, as well as through our purposeful material, research–activist engagements that aimed to foster possibilities for the children to explore, address, and communicate their experiences of harassment.

The ethical considerations in relation to the project were ongoing before, during, and after our engagements with the children. As a 'spin off' and part of Tuija's ongoing research project,[4] the #MeToo Postscriptum campaign had obtained a statement from the Ethics Committee of Human Sciences at the University of Oulu, Finland and followed the policies of the schools in all matters of child protection. The workshop participants were recruited by contacting local schools and teachers interested in participating in the campaign. Information letters and consent forms were sent to the children and their legal guardians to be signed before participation. These letters included research-based information about gender and sexual harassment as the theme of the workshops, as well as information about the creative activities of the workshops and the campaign. They also included details about the use of the produced data and the possibility that the notes could be shared publicly and in research publications. These issues were discussed again with the children in the beginning of every workshop and additionally brought up whenever it seemed important. The activist orientation of the project was materially present in the creation of the Valentine's Day cards as the children themselves chose the members of parliament to whom their cards would be sent. The children were able to withdraw at any time or negotiate their own way of participating. For example, in some of the workshops, a few of the participants created cards that they did not want to share as part of the campaign. Those cards, or any cards that were ambiguous with respect to the children's consent, were excluded from the project.

Even when carefully considering ethics as part of our praxis, engaging children in research–activism involves ongoing response-ability with respect to the project as it unfolds and, for example, becomes public. We maintain that staying with the complexities and trouble (Haraway 2008, 2012, 2016) involved is important, as the entangled constellations of research and activism can produce processes of social change and transformation both within the lives of the children and within the wider terrains of social and educational policies and practices. Particularly in relation to sexual harassment in pre-teen peer cultures, which is a silenced and often unaddressed topic in schools, asking what matters to the children themselves is important. This, along with the premise of moving beyond merely stating the state of things in research on children's peer and relationship cultures (e.g., Huuki and Renold 2016; Renold 2018), guided our research–activist aim of helping children's experiences and voices to be heard, sensed, and felt so as to cultivate conditions for co-flourishing.

Building upon the project, in this paper, we generated an analysis focusing on and departing from one of the workshops. The data are comprised of video-recordings of a workshop with eight girls, postscript notes in which the children described their experience and collaborative reflections, and personal field notes taken by the research team members. When returning to the data, our aim was not so much to gain access to some undisputable truth about the workshop. Rather, the data helped us slow down—touch, sense, feel, and think—with the material, affective, and temporal entangledness involved. Over the course of the research process—while we were engaged in the workshops, cataloguing the research materials, publishing results, and returning to the data to write this paper—the data were iterated upon, continuously reassembled, and engaged in diffractive encounters that 'pulled in' different times and spaces.

Theory is 'put to work' (Dolphijn and van der Tuin 2012) in the three analytically enacted moments—that is, moments enacted by us through agential cuts (Barad 2007) within particular,

---

[4] Project 'Gender-based violence in pre-teen relationship cultures: How history, place, affect and arts interventions matter', grant number 295000.

contingent apparatuses of knowing (see also Lenz Taguchi and Palmer 2013). In this paper, such cuts were inspired by touch. Touch, as it unfolded for us here, carries resemblance to affect, as in 'being affected'. It is also a bodily practice and a mundane moment, for example, a pen touching a paper or a hand holding a paper slip. It is these affective and material tenors of touch that invited our attention. However, informed by and diffractively engaging with Barad's ethico-onto-epistemology, discussed previously in this paper, touch became removed from its human orbit. Thus, in the three analytical sections below, we map, first, more-than-human touch focusing on the materially crowded moments within the workshops. In the second section, our focus becomes drawn to the affective charge, and we explore what else touch as a mode of material feeling and thinking does in moments of response and resistance. In the final analytical section, we focus on what else touch can become as it gathers up and holds together across time–space domains as part of our research–activism. By mapping and moving with touch, we engage touch as a more-than-human and more-than-present player that intra-actively engages in the material-discursive practices within and through which sexual harassment 'comes to matter' and, as we explore, potentially a player that engenders conditions of possibility for subtle shifts, marking and making differences that matter in the hurt, silence, normalization, and denial of gender and sexual harassment by enabling the opening up to change and transformation towards co-flourishing.

4. Research–Activist Encounters

Below, we provide two accounts of the workshop. The accounts that we offer regarding the workshop must not be understood as a set of passive props but, rather, as a space–time entangled, affectively charged environment through and within which 'what is "in" the foreground [is allowed] to acquire the shape that it does' (Ahmed 2010, pp. 239–40). In addition to describing the process of the workshop, we attune to the affective atmosphere (Stewart 2011) of the entanglements of the girls, the notes, movement, gestures, utterances, tables, chairs, and a makeshift mailbox, which will then be iterated in the following three analytical sections.

4.1. The Workshop

Similar to all the workshops, this workshop began with the children—eight girls in total—gathered in a circle of chairs. Two student teachers led the session, and Suvi participated. The student teachers read research-based statements about children's friendship and relationship cultures. Every time the participants agreed with the statement, they would stand up and switch seats. If they disagreed, or were unwilling or unable to take a stand, they would remain in place. The movement of one girl would easily stir movement in others. Sometimes, amidst bodies anchored in place to be, then again, on the move, discussions would unfold, causing us to linger on a topic for longer. Sometimes the topics would 'touch' the girls in a particular way, generating giggles or evoking stories—things the participants knew—about the ongoing relationships and romantic undercurrents within their peer relations. Those 'knowings' were sometimes voiced aloud and other times evident only in quick glances and smiles.

After the introduction to the topic of sexual harassment, the children were told about the research–activist campaign in more detail. They were instructed to craft Valentines' Day cards and, if they chose, to write about harassment they had experienced. Slips of paper with examples of some of the experiences disclosed in previous workshops with young people were put on the wall to prompt reflection. The notes described contentious and troubling touches and experiences with just a few words or a sentence, such as 'I have been slapped on the butt' or 'some boys in our class groped between girls' thighs with a ruler'.

Soon, the children began to collect materials to create their Valentine's Day cards. They gathered in a close group around one of the tables, chatting while they cut and folded the base of the cards and decorated them with drawings, tapes, stamps, glitter glue, and colors. When the cards were nearly ready and the participants began to contemplate their postscripts, the atmosphere shifted. If they had previously been gathered together, they seemed to scatter around the classroom, taking their newly crafted cards or empty slips of paper with them. For some of the children, it seemed difficult to think of something to write. This was expected, as not all children are caught up in same ways within the flows of peer and relationship cultures. Others hunched over their cards to shelter the affective, intimate, precarious space in which their experiences of harassment could be safely figured in words, written down, attached to the card, and eventually, slipped into a makeshift mailbox that was set up on one of the tables. Once placed in the mailbox, the notes and cards became part of the campaign. Some of them were curated for publishing online, and all of them were mailed to decisionmakers.

Gradually, the workshop session came to a close as the children left the classroom to get lunch, leaving the research team with the video recordings and the to-be-written research notes, the box of cards, and lingering affects—as we will elaborate upon below—which became reassembled within the broader research–activist apparatus of change-making regarding sexual harassment (Pihkala and Huuki 2019).

4.2. A Girl with a Note

In the latter half of the workshop, one girl caught Suvi's attention. At this point, the girl had already put her Valentine's Day card in the makeshift mailbox. She was one of the first participants to finish her card, but it did not include a postscript. Suvi remembered telling her that this was okay, as we could use such cards if someone else had several bits of stories to share. After completing the activity, she returned to the table where the others were still making their cards. Later, the girl began to meander around the room, walking from one table to the next and looking at the arts and crafts on the tables. We do not know what made her get up. Perhaps she was prompted by the fact that others had begun to find more private spaces to write, or perhaps the request to share experiences was made more insistent by the movement of bodies and shift in attention.

The girl halted by one of the tables, on which we had spread the notes that were previously hung on the wall to evoke discussion and reflection. She continued on but returned, pausing a bit longer by the table and whispering with another girl who had joined her there. Having looked at the notes for a while, the girl asked, 'Could one write something like that?' as she pointed to one of the notes. Suvi confirmed that she could and encouraged her to write something down if she still wanted to. Without saying much more, she took an empty slip of paper, returned to the table where she had been before, and began to write.

Moments later, the girl rose and walked to the makeshift mailbox, clutching the paper note, which was a little less than half the size of an A4 paper, close to her chest. Then, carefully doubling the paper without folding it, as if to keep her writing sheltered from others, she reached towards the makeshift mailbox and slipped her note in. She stepped to the side, looked back at the box and then walked away, hands casually in her jumper pockets, but it felt that what just happened was anything but casual.

After the workshop ended and we returned to our office to catalogue the cards, Suvi noticed that very same paper note, remembering the color and size. She remembered how the girl moved and halted at the table, the pointing, the card, and the curve of the note as she slipped it into the makeshift mailbox. All the details were pulled into that moment of recognition in the office. In her note, which, as part of the campaign, became entangled in the wider mosaic of experiences of harassment, the girl shared her painful experience from a few years back. Even though she sheltered the note from the eyes of her classmates, her slipping it into the makeshift mailbox, instead of the cards to be excluded from the project, gestured perhaps a political moment and movement of speaking out. We have not identified her experience in its singularity to ensure the girl's anonymity and because our focus is not on the experience described on the note but, rather, on the microprocesses of change and the subtle shifts that unfolded within and through the workshop. However, to respect this movement from silence to speaking out and speaking up, we have elsewhere made parts of the children's notes public (see Huuki and Pihkala 2018; Pihkala and Huuki 2019).

5. Past–Present Child–Card Entanglements of Response-Ability

In this section, we map touch through the three analytically enacted moments. Each section, while entangled in nature, draws attention in specific ways to the productivity of the materiality, affective charge, and movements across time–space domains, as has been elaborated previously.

5.1. Mapping Touch as More-Than-Human

The design of the workshops—its different modalities and creative activities, as elaborated previously in this paper; the size and composition of the group; and the attention to more-than-human—were co-constructed so as to enable an atmosphere that 'touches' enough to enable 'responsiveness', that is, to help children explore, communicate, and address experiences of harassment that easily tend to be overcast by deafening silence when addressed in the primary school classroom. During the workshop, the girls gathered together, moved about, and stayed still while crafting with papers, pens, glitter glue, tapes, and colors. The notes laid out on the table carried traces of experiences of harassment, connecting the workshop to the collective history of felt and sensed touches of sexual harassment, be it physical, verbal, or otherwise, enfolded in this entanglement of child-bodies, notes, circles, tables, and the campaign. This intra-action of bodies, movements, and materials opening up to the unexpected and emergent is our first analytical cut.

For Barad (2014), touching is not centered on a human being, nor is it only affective. It is ontological and epistemological. Touching is what matter does. With this understanding of touch, the girls' movements and haltings, rummaging through the arts and crafts materials, writing and drawing, and re-membering (Barad 2010) past experiences fail to return to any one individual alone. Similar to the girl with the pointed finger tentatively asking if it could be 'something like that', the 'it' that comes to matter fails to return to an individual imagination or recognition only. Rather, within the intra-active entanglement of glitter glue, colors, paper slips, past-presents, and engaged bodies—sitting and moving in a circle and sharing experiences—it is not only the girls that touch and are touched. Thinking along the lines of Barad, both the girls and the matter—things, moments, and places—wander and wonder, curiously sensing and touching their im/possibilities, imagining, and inventing (Barad 2014, 2015).

In these moments of moving, halting, inciting, and inviting human and other than human bodies, matter, in its curious and imaginative 'self-touching' form (Barad 2014), reconfigures the girls' experiences for recognition in new ways. As bodies move within the circle of chairs; smiles appear; pens touch paper; bodies shift and sway in proximity and distance; gazes fall on notes; and past experiences make themselves present, touches subtly shift and rework hurtful, painful, unaddressed, and deep-seated experiences—even an experience from two years ago—for recognition, bringing something within reach that was not present before and perhaps reachable in a way that was not possible before.

5.2. What Else Touch Can Do: The Affective Charge in Response and Resistance

Our second analytical moment enacts a cut that draws focus to the affective charge in the intra-action of notes, bodies, and a makeshift mailbox. We return to the girl who clutched the note to her chest, carefully sheltering it from others, while also sharing it with others once she slipped it into the makeshift mailbox on the table. In the affectively charged mo(ve)ment of this 'held-shared' note from the intimacy of the girl's chest to the public space of the makeshift mailbox, being touched does something else; it reconfigures conditions of possibilities for touching in response.

When we returned to and re-engaged with this moment, we were caught by its force, as well as by our own visceral responses during the campaign. To elaborate, we had set up a pop-up stand in the university café to engage student teachers and faculty members in the campaign. The pop-up stand enabled passers-by to craft their own Valentine's Day cards and include their stories of harassment during childhood as postscripts. While sitting by a table in a busy café, we also wrote down our experiences. More than once, we found ourselves confronted with the difficulty and discomfort of doing so. An array of charges passed through our bodies: who sees me; who passes by; who sees the painful experience that comes to matter and is made to matter in this moment. We understand such charges as sensed-felt resonances and dissonance between the sensitivity of the experience, deep-seated anxieties related to our experiences of harassment and abuse, and the publicity both in that moment and inherent in the promise of the campaign, which invited us to explore intimate experiences and make them matter for others. It is through those embodied affective encounters and similar experiences shared by colleagues that we began to speculate about the ways the intra-active moment with the girl, the note, the moving–holding hands, and the makeshift mailbox was iteratively reconfigured from within the material and affective entanglements of the research–activist campaign.

As we sensed-felt while writing our own notes about harassment, in this moment, with the girl and the note and the materiality and affects of our research–activist workshop, touch was a sensed-felt resonance that intra-acted with the cards, the pens, the tables, the public space of the café, the passing bodies, and the rhythm of academic work and time and opened up towards a possible other world, generating new patterns of diffraction. Perhaps this touch is what Hemmings (2012) calls affective dissonance, the incongruity of ontology and epistemology and of being and knowing, which is felt as a visceral force, such as uncertainty, shame, upset, decidedness, and courage. This force marks the sense and feel of something coming within reach that was not there before in a way that invites engagement. For Hemmings (2012, p. 151), it is such dissonances that hold political possibility and the promise of movement. The movement within this entanglement of the girl—and, indeed, us as well—the note, and the embodied practice of holding the note close while reaching towards the makeshift mailbox unfolds as a mo(ve)ment of response, response-ability, and resistance.

We contend that what touch as a more-than-human player does in this moment is that it co-constitutes a site and space of response—a space enfolded with affects, things, places, and moments and unfolding towards resistance. Amplified by our own responses to writing down our pasts, we understand that the ability to be moved and affected to reach in resistance and to disturb the norms of what can be said, what can be resisted, what can be disrupted—be it the heterosexist normativities or intra-generational trauma (Huuki and Lanas 2019)—is frail and precarious. Yet, we maintain that the intra-active entanglement of the cards, the words written in the postscripts, the makeshift mailbox, and the promise and possibility of action enfolded in it allowed the past experience of hurt—the recognition—to reconfigure and to be not only known but to be resisted.

5.3. What Else Touch Can Become: Gathering Up and Holding Together/Apart across Time–Space Domains

As we curated the cards for the campaign website, the note became reanimated, making sense-able the response-ability and accountability it crafted by inviting and obliging us to care about it and to be careful with it without certainty if the 'it' is the card, the 'data', the words written in the cards, the girl who wrote it, the upsetting experience described in the note, the hurt embedded within it, or perhaps the academic writing about 'it'. The intra-active entanglement of the child, cards, creative practice, research, and activism diffracts, sending out ripples that, no matter how small, hold the potentiality for 'consequential meanings' (Haraway 1997). This touch of the girl's response held its grip when we selected excerpts from the cards to publish on the campaign website and when the upset and hurt became realigned in the title of a news article in a national newspaper, (re-)making us as (modest) witnesses, complicit, and response-able (Haraway 1997, 2008). For Haraway (2008, p. 36), this is exactly what touches can do: they shape and ramify accountability, where '[a]ccountability, caring for, being affected, and entering into responsibility are not ethical abstractions' but mundane practices of becoming with.

As explored earlier in this paper, due to the affective charge sensed and felt by us while writing notes about our childhood experiences of harassment, there was a familiarity that resonated from the entanglement of the girl, the note, and the makeshift mailbox. It would be rather easy to foreground how we were emotionally affected by the girl's story and how the touch–affect jumps back and forth, first during the workshop and again in the office, from us to the girl and from the girl to us or to all those 'others' who we can imagine being touched. Perhaps it was the familiarity in the dissonance of holding close and disclosing that we recognize, of keeping hidden but wanting to seize the opportunity to disrupt conventional silences around touches that hurt—to reach and touch in resistance.

The sense of familiarity moves us to speculate that we were not merely slightly grazed by this one experience and the touches surrounding it; rather, in being touched by the girl's experience, matter, time, and space realigned and reinvented itself in a reiterative practice of reconfiguring (Barad 2007). In effect, we argue that touch, as mapped here, reaches and holds across and beyond space–time domains. Our adult researcher bodies hold and carry 'impressions' of our own past touches—such as a re-membered slap—which, as Barad (2010) notes, never left us. New touches stick to us, such as the touch–affect from the girl. These touches did not just stick and jump but became more-than-human and more-than-present players in this research–activist constellation. Each touch invents new matter forms by gathering up and holding together/apart the past and present (Barad 2010), the researcher-adult, the researcher-child, the girl with the note, the researcher with a note, and, perhaps, also the pre-teen girls that have been and will be affected by sexual harassment in their peer relations.

Neither the girl being touched nor we, who were being touched by the girl-being-touched, were contained in the 'touch-encounter'. Thinking along the lines of Barad (2007), we enter into relations of response not because of what touches us from afar but because there were never separate parts to begin with. Indeed, response-abilities are not crafted from a graze. In other words, they are not created by 'knowing' the girl's troubling experience but from the capacity of us be(com)ing (with) in touch (see Pihkala 2018), that is, the capacity of touch to draw times, spaces, and matter into new relations, inviting touch in response.

6. Microprocesses of Change and the Possibilities of Moving with Touch

Knowing what we know and feeling what we feel, any of the notes from our research–activist campaign might be swarming with as many affects, times, and embodied materiality as surround the workshop or the girl with the note as discussed in this paper. Nonetheless, in this particular entangled practice of engagement, this girl touched us, took hold of us, and pulled us to move with touch in response. Furthermore, slipped into the makeshift mailbox, the girls' notes, 'crafted from and carrying their experience' (Renold 2018, p. 38), became 'knotted' with the wider change-making apparatus against sexual harassment: the campaigns, personal accounts, public debate, and (digital) feminist activism that have enabled young people to speak out against 'rape culture' in new ways (Mendes et al. 2018). To claim how the campaign mattered to the girls—or any of the participants—would be speculative at best. However, the children's need to address and explore their concerns related to gender and sexual peer cultures has been tangible time and time again as the children have voiced the need for safe spaces where sensitive topics could be discussed. For this, engaging children with creative activities can enable subtle shifts and minor gestures (Manning 2016) towards sustainable alternatives in peer relations when imagined worlds are materialized through crafting, drawing, and writing.

The research–activist encounters of our creative workshop against sexual harassment in pre-teen peer cultures is materially rich, affectively charged, and temporally entangled. In gauging the microprocesses of change as they occur, we mapped touch and explored what else touch(es) can do. As we mapped in our analysis, the entanglement of the group of girls, Valentine's Day cards, past, and present involved different kinds of touches in different registers, such as embodied, *corporeal touches* of gropes and slaps; verbal touches; material touches of pen on paper; present touches that leave impressions and linger; past touches that carry the residues of the past; the touch–affects that slip through cognition shooting straight through our bodies in resonances and dissonances; and the onto-epistemological touches that sense the virtual in an exploration of the possible, quantum, and queer touches, as discussed by Barad (2015). Just as touch seems to settle in senses, it is already on the move, reaching, holding, and gathering. The childhood slaps and gropes reached the Valentine's Day cards in a café, the child-bodies reached a researcher-child, a finger reached for a pile of notes, a hand reached for the makeshift mailbox, the mailbox reached us, and the otherwise-made-possible reached the body-in-reach.

We maintain that there is a particular benefit in thinking of the microprocesses of change with touch. For one, mapping touch, as we did here, enabled us to capture the subtle shifts in the children's unaddressed, silenced, normalized, hurtful experience. Rather than being here and there—or this or that—touches intra-acted within and through the workshop as more-than-human and more-than-present players and converged into an inventive, imaginative, sensing-feeling, matter-realizing apparatus, which activated recognition of, response to, and resistance against sexualized and gendered force relations. Thinking along the lines of Barad (2014), this is what touch—when thought of in the quantum mode—can do: sense and feel and gather up and hold together/apart (Barad 2014, 2015). Drawing matter into new relations, characterized by indeterminacy waiting to remake momentary alliances, touch reworks and recrafts response-abilities (Barad 2014; Haraway 2008).

For another, the ethico-political tone of touch is intimate and entangled. With touch, it is impossible to keep one's distance or disavow how we are touched and how the ways we touch shape and co-constitute the conditions of possibilities for touching in response and resistance to the 'other'. Our experience of being touched by the girls' experiences and our research–activism, which brought disparate matters and modalities together, generating the imaginative, creative, sensing-feeling apparatus, knotted us in webs of manifold more-than-human and more-than-present touches that diffractively reconfigured ever-new possibilities for change. For us, as researchers and activists, thinking with touch engages theory in ways that moves and transforms relations, engagements, and accountabilities. We contend that this is the way feminist new materialist touch works: it is not only 'put to work' (Dolphijn and van der Tuin 2012) but becomes enacted when objects, bodies, abstractions, and moments intra-act—how they sense and feel, imagine and invent, reach in response, gather up, and hold together.

Finally, thinking about our research–activism with touch draws attention to the affective, material, and temporally entangled encounters that contest and remake what is possible, producing 'differences that matter'. While the anatomy of these encounters cannot be laid bare, engaging them with new conceptual companions—as we did in this paper—can help enrich the ways we think, feel, and practice research in ways that can make a difference. Indeed, moving with touch aligns with more-than-theoretical approaches to what research can do. It speaks to the power and potentiality of and responsibility to participate in co-composing research encounters that invite and enable response to the other. This demands that we carefully co-compose thick, material, and affective encounters that invite and enable children, researchers, and others to sense, feel, think, imagine, wander, and wonder with—to become with (Haraway 2008)—the postscripts, cards, pens, papers, space, and time and, through subtle shifts, make new kinds of, more livable, worlds.

To close with a tentative gesture, mapping what touches do encouraged us to also imagine a touch that is of a world-making kind (Haraway 2008) and one that creates accountability and response-ability (Barad 2014). With this, we maintain that moving with touch is an open-ended endeavor but one imbued with conviction. Touch not only brings other beings, spaces, and times together (or to matter) but also leaks out to other worlds by reaching in response and resistance, touching and carefully holding those other visions, worlds, and possibilities. At the same time, we are not left untouched; as we reach out, response and resistance stick to us.

Author Contributions: Conceptualization, S.P. and T.H.; Investigation, S.P. and T.H.; Methodology, S.P. and T.H.; Writing—original draft, S.P.; Writing—review & editing, T.H. and V.S.

Funding: This research was partly funded by Academy of Finland, grant number 295000.

Acknowledgments: We would like to acknowledge communal and visual artist Anna Koivukangas for suggesting the title #MeToo Postscriptum to us when we were planning the project. We wish to thank the student teachers involved in the workshops as well as the teachers and most importantly the children and schools without whom the #MeToo Postscriptum would not have been possible.

Conflicts of Interest: The authors declare no conflicts of interest.

References

Ahmed, Sara. 2010. Orientations Matter. In *New Materialisms: Ontology, Agency, and Politics*. Edited by Diana Coole and Samantha Frost. Durham: Duke University Press, pp. 234–57.

Barad, Karen. 2007. *Meeting the Universe Halfway: Quantum Physics and the Entanglement of Matter and Meaning*. Durham: Duke University Press.

Barad, Karen. 2010. Quantum Entanglements and Hauntological Relations of Inheritance: Dis/continuities, Spacetime Enfoldings, and Justice-to-Come. *Derrida Today* 3: 240–68. [CrossRef]

Barad, Karen. 2014. On Touching—The Inhuman That Therefore I Am (v1.1). In *The Power of Material—The Politics of Materiality*. Edited by Susanne Witzgall and Kerstin Stakemeier. Zurich: Diaphanes, pp. 153–64.

Barad, Karen. 2015. Transmaterialities: Trans*/matter/realities and Queer Political Imaginings. *GLQ: A Journal of Lesbian and Gay Studies* 21: 387–422. [CrossRef]

Blackman, Lisa, and Couze Venn. 2010. Affect. *Body and Society* 16: 7–28. [CrossRef]

Braidotti, Rosi. 2013. *The Posthuman*. Cambridge: Edinburgh University Press.

Dolphijn, Rick, and Iris van der Tuin. 2012. *New Materialism: Interviews & Cartographies*. Ann Arbor: Open Humanities Press. [CrossRef]

Fox, Nick J., and Pam Alldred. 2016. *Sociology and the New Materialism. Theory, Research, Action*. Los Angeles: Sage.

Gillander Gådin, Katja. 2012. Sexual Harassment of Girls in Elementary School a Concealed Phenomenon within a Heterosexual Romantic Discourse. *Journal of Interpersonal Violence* 27: 1762–79. [CrossRef] [PubMed]

Haraway, Donna. 1997. *Modest_Witness@Second_millenium.FemaleMan©_Meets_OncoMouse™*. London: Routledge.

Haraway, Donna. 2008. *When Species Meet*. Minneapolis: Minnesota University Press.

Haraway, Donna. 2012. Awash in Urine: DES and Premarin® in Multispecies Response-Ability. *WQS: Women's Quaterly* 1–2: 301–17. [CrossRef]

Haraway, Donna. 2016. *Staying with the Trouble: Making Kin in the Chthulucene*. Durham: Duke University Press.

Hemmings, Clare. 2012. Affective Solidarity: Feminist Reflexivity and Political Transformation. *Feminist Theory* 13: 147–61. [CrossRef]

Holford, Naomi, Emma Renold, and Tuija Huuki. 2013. What (Else) Can a Kiss Do?: Theorizing the Power Plays in Young Children's Sexual Cultures. *Sexualities* 6: 710–29. [CrossRef]

Huuki, Tuija, Sari Manninen, and Vappu Sunnari. 2010. Humour as a Resource and Strategy for Boys to Gain Status in the Field of Informal School. *Gender and Education* 22: 369–83. [CrossRef]

Huuki, Tuija, and Emma Renold. 2016. Crush: Mapping Historical, Material and Affective Force Relations in Young Children's Hetero-Sexual Playground Play. *Discourse: Studies in the Cultural Politics of Education* 37: 754–69. [CrossRef]

Huuki, Tuija, and Suvi Pihkala. 2018. #MeToo Postscriptum. Available online: https://metoopostscript.wordpress.com/ (accessed on 5 July 2019).

Huuki, Tuija, and Maija Lanas. 2019. Sámi Child-Adult/past-Present Entanglements in a Painful Lecture in University. In *Social, Material and Political Constructs of Arctic Childhoods: An Everyday Life Perspective*. Edited by Pauliina Rautio and Elina Stenvall. Singapore: Springer, pp. 135–48.

Huuki, Tuija. 2019. Collaging the Virtual: Gender Materialisations in the Artwork of Pre-Teen Children. *Childhood*. [CrossRef]

Lenz Taguchi, Hillevi, and Anna Palmer. 2013. A more 'livable' school? A diffractive analysis of the performative enactments of girls' ill-/well-being with(in) school environments. *Gender and Education* 25: 671–87. [CrossRef]

Manning, Erin. 2016. *The Minor Gesture*. Durham: Duke University Press.

Massumi, Brian. 2015. *Politics of Affect*. Cambridge: Polity.

Mendes, Kaitlynn, Jessica Ringrose, and Jessalynn Keller. 2018. #MeToo and the Promise and Pitfalls of Challenging Rape Culture through Digital Feminist Activism. *European Journal of Women's Studies* 25: 236–46. [CrossRef]

Meyer, Elizabeth J. 2009. *Gender, Bullying, and Harassment: Strategies to End Sexism and Homophobia in Schools*. New York: Teachers College Press.

Pihkala, Suvi. 2018. Touchable Matters: Reconfiguring Sustainable Change Through Participatory Design, Education and Everyday Engagement for Non-Violence. Doctoral dissertation, University of Oulu, Oulu, Finland, April 6. Available online: http://urn.fi/urn:isbn:9789526218434 (accessed on 25 July 2019).

Pihkala, Suvi, Tuija Huuki, Mervi Heikkinen, and Vappu Sunnari. 2018. Reconfigurings of Non-Violence as a Matter of Response-Ability and Sustainability. *NORA—Nordic Journal of Feminist and Gender Research* 26: 167–81. [CrossRef]

Pihkala, Suvi, and Tuija Huuki. 2019. How a Hashtag Matters—Crafting Response(-Abilities) through Creative Research-Activism Addressing Sexual Harassment in Pre-Teen Peer Cultures. Unpublished manuscript.

Renold, Emma. 2013. *Boys and Girls Speak Out: A Qualitative Study of Children's Gender and Sexual Cultures (Ages 10–12)*. Cardiff: Cardiff University, Available online: http://www.childcom.org.uk/uploads/publications/411.pdf (accessed on 25 July 2019).

Renold, Emma. 2018. "Feel What I Feel": Making Da(r)ta with Teen Girls for Creative Activisms on How Sexual Violence Matters. *Journal of Gender Studies* 27: 37–55. [CrossRef]

Renold, Emma. 2019. Becoming AGENDA: Co-creating of a youth-activist resource to address gendered and sexual violence with a run-a-way pARTicipatory praxis. An unpublished manuscript.

Renold, Emma, and Jessica Ringrose. 2019. JARing: Making phematerialist research practices matter. *MAI: Feminism and Visual Culture*, May 16. Available online: https://maifeminism.com/introducing-phematerialism-feminist-posthuman-and-new-materialist-research-methodologies-in-education/ (accessed on 25 July 2019).

Ringrose, Jessica, Katie Warfield, and Shiva Zarabadi. 2019. Introducing Feminist Posthumanisms/New Materialisms & Educational Research: Response-able Theory-Practice-Methodology. In *Feminist Posthumanisms, New Materialisms, and Education*. Edited by Ringrose Jessica, Katie Warfield and Shiva Zarabadi. London: Routledge, pp. 1–15.

Stein, Nan. 2007. Locating a Secret Problem: Sexual Violence in Elementary and Secondary Schools. In *Gender Violence: Interdisciplinary Perspectives*, 2nd ed. Edited by Laura O'Toole, Jessica R. Schiffman and Margie L. Kitter Edwards. New York: New York University Press, pp. 323–32.

Stewart, Kathleen. 2011. Atmospheric Attunements. *Environment and Planning D: Society and Space* 29: 445–53. [CrossRef]

Sunnari, Vappu. 2010. *"I Cannot Speak about It". Physical Sexual Harassment as Experienced by Children at School in Northern Finland and Northwest Russia*. Saarbrücken: VDM Verlag.

Sunnari, Vappu, Jenny Kangasvuo, and Mervi Heikkinen, eds. 2002. *Gendered and Sexualised Violence in Educational Environments*, 2nd ed. Oulu: Oulu University Press, Available online: http://herkules.oulu.fi/isbn9514268946/isbn9514268946.pdf (accessed on 25 July 2019).

Taylor, Carol A. 2018. Each Intra-Action Matters: Towards a Posthuman Ethics for Enlarging Response-Ability in Higher Education Pedagogic Practice-Ings. In *Socially Just Pedagogies: Posthumanist, Feminist and Materialist Perspectives in Higher Education*. Edited by Rosi Braidotti, Vivienne Bozalek, Tamara Shefer and Michalinos Zembylas. London: Bloomsbury, pp. 81–96.

© 2019 by the authors. Licensee MDPI, Basel, Switzerland. This article is an open access article distributed under the terms and conditions of the Creative Commons Attribution (CC BY) license (http://creativecommons.org/licenses/by/4.0/).

Article

New Materialist Feminist Ecological Practices: La Via Campesina and Activist Environmental Work

Miranda Imperial

Department of Media and Communications, London School of Economics and Political Science, London WC2A 2AE, UK; miranda.imperial@gmail.com

Received: 2 May 2019; Accepted: 6 August 2019; Published: 8 August 2019

Abstract: Within the context of new theoretical developments in environmentalist materialism, as inflected by gender issues, this paper attempts to analyze the important work of La Via Campesina (women's section) both in grassroots activism and in creating a feminist agenda for the transformation of human-non-human connections. Methodologically, this paper proceeds by historically situating La Via Campesina and the progressive incorporation of women's issues as part of the movement. In parallel, La Via Campesina's insurgent practices of contestation to the exploitation of huge multinational agrobusinesses, to genetically modified crops, and to land-grabbing practices and land usurpation from indigenous populations are illustrated. In conclusion and within the frame of new materialisms, my discussion addresses issues of response-ability, sustainability, and co-habitation to reflect upon the major changes brought about by these new modes of thinking and inhabiting the planet.

Keywords: new materialisms; feminist environmentalism; ecology; grassroots activism; La Via Campesina; political ecology; response-ability; food sovereignty; social justice

1. Introduction

The new relational basis between humans, living and inert matter, technology, and the planet that the new materialisms are proposing is a growing reality that can be observed in many domains, from epistemology to anthropology, ecology, and ethics. It is precisely at the crossroads of ecology and the political that this paper is situated, and it aims to explore how in and through the practice of feminist new materialisms, political ecology, and grassroots activist organizing, significant changes can be brought about to prevent irreversible damage such as climate change, or to eradicate dumping industrial waste into rivers and oceans and to eliminate chemicals and plastic residue from food, shelter, and the daily existence of life on the planet.

Framed within recent developments in the field of feminist perspectives on the environment, my paper will examine a major feminist, political, and environmental project, La Via Campesina's gendered initiative, which exists within the larger context of the struggle of La Via Campesina, in order to reflect upon the political valences both in grassroots activism and in new ecological insurgent practices in which women have become actively involved. It is my contention that currently, La Via Campesina participates of the ethos and concerns of feminist new materialisms, and I will attempt to demonstrate their proximity and similar goals. After an introduction to the most relevant work in new materialist views on the environment which pave the way to my argument, I will address how La Via Campesina came to consider women's social, economic, and labor issues as central to the movement and identify La Via Campesina's major claims and demands in relation to agriculture and agrarian reform. Tenets such as the achievement of food sovereignty for peasants and indigenous populations in their plight against huge multinational agrobusinesses interact with other crucial principles which I will spell out. At those levels, women's labor is indispensable for the maintenance and continuation of community life. La Via Campesina's gendered insurgent practices will also be analyzed as a response to the deleterious effects which the overexploitation, pollution, and land-grabbing effects produced by late capitalism have had on human and nonhuman actors alike. Finally, and within the framework of new materialisms, I will briefly address issues of response-ability, sustainability, and co-habitation in the planet as parts of the common ground that trans-species engagement,[1] posthumanism, and new modes of thinking and inhabiting the world have brought to our attention. As it has been pointed out, the assumption of one world or one universe is inherently colonial in that "it sustains itself through performances that tend to suppress and or contain the enactment of other possible worlds" (Blaser 2009, p. 16). For Blaser, the idea of the pluriverse is a more adequate concept because it entails imagining the performative enactment of multiple, distinct ontologies or worlds which "bring themselves into being and sustain themselves even as they interact, interfere and mingle with each other" (Blaser 2012, p. 55) under asymmetrical circumstances.

The changing pattern of action between the nation-state and rural organizations at the beginning of the 1980s with progressively more detached policies and a worsening of conditions in the countryside brought about an acute social awareness of endemic problems within peasant organizations. This state of affairs and the peasants' conviction that major obstacles in their work and daily lives had to do with wider oppressive conditions beyond the national borders of ever weakened nation-states is at the origin of La Via Campesina as a transnational social movement. During the 1980s and early 1990s, La Via Campesina emerged out of autonomous peasant organizations first in Latin America and then at a global scale. By being organized globally, in defense of their interests and to protect their working conditions and ways of life, their members seek to advocate a reasonable and sustainable agrarian production which takes as its basis a holistic approach of interaction between the land and its communities. This grassroots organization has become enormously influential in setting up agendas for sensitive agrarian reform and social policies worldwide. According to Martinez-Torres and Rosset, "La Via Campesina today is the leading network of grassroots organizations with presence in the anti-globalization or altermundista ('another world') movement, as manifested in protests against the World Trade Organization (WTO) and Free Trade Area of the Americas (FTAA), in the World Social Forum (WSF), in its scathing techniques of World Bank land policies and its ability to force the novel concept of food sovereignty into common usage" (Martinez-Torres and Rosset 2010, p. 151).

This paper aims to contribute to a better understanding of the specific actions of the transnational movement La Via Campesina and their proximity to feminist new materialist developments. Methodologically, I have first approached La Via historically in order to show when peasant women start getting organized within the movement. Secondly, I have analyzed three specific actions relevant in three major areas: opposition to large agribusiness corporations, predatory exploitation of water resources, and land-grabbing and farmers' dispossession. These were chosen among other actions because they were carried out by South American (Brazilian and Argentinian) peasant women who were all members of the Peasant without Land movements, and because they are among the most publicized of these actions, as judged by their Internet presence (Google). In my analysis, I have attempted to demonstrate how these actions can be read by recourse to new materialist ideas and concepts.

2. The Challenges of Ecological Feminism

In recent years, philosophy, feminisms, environmental studies, and biotechnology have alerted people to the current state of degradation of the planet. Contemporary eco-feminist thinking finds its roots in the second wave of feminism, back in the 1970s. In northern India, in the early 70s, many

---

[1] It was anthropologist Eduardo Kohn who coined the idea of "trans-species engagement." In his view, "[c]reating an analytical framework that can include the humans as well as non-humans has been a central concern of science and technology studies, the multispecies or animal turn, and Deleuze-influenced scholarship [...] And I have been specially swayed by Donna Haraway's conviction that there is something about our everyday engagements with other kinds of creatures that can open new kinds of possibilities for relating and understanding" (Kohn 2013, pp. 6–7).

women took part in the Chipko movement to protect forests from commercial loggers and deforestation. Throughout the 1980s important initiatives spread around the globe, and native American and indigenous women were thought to be the ultimate ecofeminists. The origins of the early Indian feminist green movement can be traced to social critic Vandana Shiva. In her view, Indian women have an inherent connection to nature. She speaks of the "feminine principle," insisting on the fact that this has nothing to do with an outdated notion of matriarchy but rather with an idea of gender complementarity in sexual divisions of labor. She writes:

> In this non-gender based philosophy the feminine principle is not exclusively embodied in women, but is the principle of activity and creativity in nature, women and men. One cannot really distinguish the masculine from the feminine, person from nature, Purusha from Praktiri. Though distinct, they remain inseparable in dialectical unity, as two aspects of one being. (Shiva 1989, p. 52)

Clearly, Shiva's orientation was essentialist and her work came under strong criticism. However, her ideas were crucial in challenging the hegemony of scientific knowledge in the hands of men and in promoting "global sisterhood" around environmental issues. Also involved in a movement countering deforestation in Australia, and after significant activist work, Val Plumwood became a very influential voice in feminist environmentalism. In *Feminism and the Mastery of Nature* (Plumwood 1993), Plumwood argues we live in a progressively dystopic world where:

> [T]echnological mastery extinguishes both nature and less technologically "rational" cultures, where we face the imminent prospect of loss of the world's forests along with the bulk of its species diversity as well as human and cultural diversity [...] where the dominance of rational man threatens ultimately to produce the most irrational of results, the extinction of our species along with many others. (Plumwood 1993, p. 7)

Ecological feminism identifies this catastrophe as derived from a world dominated by men. In the 1990s Plumwood urged us to move beyond divisions within the women's movements and join forces to counter the destruction of the planet. She proposes alternatives to rationality "which encourage[d] mutually sustaining relationships between humans and the earth" (Plumwood 1993, p. 195). Her important program for the transformation of those relations involves "creating a democratic culture beyond dualism, ending colonizing relationships and finding a mutual, ethical basis for enriching coexistence with earth others" (Plumwood 1993, p. 196). Plumwood's important ecological agenda shows respect for alterity and grounds ethical responsibility at the core of human-non-human interactions. The engagement of activists, academics, philosophers, and large numbers of women and inhabitants of the planet has progressively grown into a global green movement with local specificities.

Conclusive findings in sociological research into the late capitalist use of resources and in human adaptation to rapid and definitive changes on Earth urge both the world population and our political representatives to work actively to counter this dismal state of affairs. A call for new forms of ethics and politics has emerged in an effort to counter the destructive, exploitative practices and lethal power upon human and non-human actors in the Anthropocene (Tsing et al. 2017).[2] Along this line, fresh insight from "Anthropocene feminism" reaches audiences critically with an impulse attentive to global change connected to ecological transformations, technological development, inequitable sharing of the resources for co-existence, and political contestation and resistance. As Claire Colebrook states:

> The proposed (and close to consecrated) conception of the Anthropocene epoch appears to mark as radical a shift in species awareness as Darwinian evolution effected for the

---

[2] Our currently used notion of the Anthropocene comes from assessing the impact of human settlement, labour, exchange, and other related activities on the planet. The human impact on geology and ecosystems translates into a huge transformation of all other forms of life on Earth. Establishing the beginning of this era is not an easy task but there is a tendency to speak of the Agricultural Revolution, 15,000 years back in time, as a major historical milestone (Tsing et al. 2017).

nineteenth century. If the notion of the human species' emergence in time requires new forms of narrative, and imaginative and ethical articulation, then the intensifying sense of the species' end makes a similar claim for rethinking "our" processes of self-presentation and self-preservation. (Colebrook 2017, p. 1)

The aforementioned problems, closely related to the life/death divide, highlight the inherent contradiction of early feminist theorists that signified what Stacy Alaimo has referred to as the "feminist flight from nature" (Alaimo 2000): the feminist abhorrence of traditional patriarchal metaphors associating women and nature. However, such views resulted from a lack of awareness and engagement in key issues regarding the environment and the current stage of scientific work on the border between the biological and social sciences (Haraway 1991, pp. 184–85), which have, nonetheless, been brought to the forefront by new feminist initiatives on science, postcolonial and decolonial theory, and new materialist philosophy, and have had a crucial impact on the way these disciplines interact and draw from each other's findings. These initiatives, summarized by Garvey (2014), attempt to undermine traditional nature/culture binarisms from different angles, and mention should be made of: Rosi Braidotti's "nomadic subjects/ethics" (Braidotti 2013), and "posthumanism" (Braidotti 2013); Nancy Tuana's "viscous porosity" and "interactionism" (Tuana 2008); Karen Barad's "intra-actionism" (Barad 2007) and "posthumanist performativity" (Barad 2008); Donna Haraway's "naturecultures" (Haraway 2008), "material-semiotic" (Haraway 1997), cyborg (Haraway 1991), and "companion species" (Haraway 2008); and Stacy Alaimo's "transcorporeality" (Alaimo 2008). These concepts help not only to move feminisms forward, but also suggest possible interventions within the material, social, and political domains affecting the world at large. In the political arena, it is crucial that decisions come to be discussed in the open and are the object of participatory democracy, and are no longer debatable by lobbies or by the elite. These proposals do not simply come as a consequence of intersectional feminism[3] (often, "intersectional" is only relevant to human lives) but, rather, are interactionist-oriented.

3. New Materialist Environmentalisms

It can certainly be stated that our current understanding of the environment has substantially changed in the last three decades. The opening statement of the Paris 2017 Conference on "Environmental Humanities and New Materialisms" announced that these two areas "share an ethic of decolonizing nature and culture, as they depart from anthropocentric and constructivist positions. Our call is to consider ourselves as permeable, part of the ebb and flow of the Anthropocene ... " (Barrett et al. 2017). The conference urged us to adopt an "environmentally ethical sense of matter within a world caught in the throes of change" (Barrett et al. 2017). The shared materiality of all living entities in the planet and their recently recognized sense of connectivity[4] provides a basis for the acknowledgement of differences, an urge to respect the specificities of elements in their localities, and initiatives to preserve, and also to restore the catastrophic consequences of the systematic erosion and devastation of our habitats.

If we turn to Judith Butler's important work on vulnerability, it is fundamental to listen to her caveat that the condition of vulnerability and the hazards of exposure to potential danger or threat

---

[3] Critical race theorist Kimberlé Crenshaw (1989) was one of the earliest proponents of intersectionality when she pointed out the inability of a single Western feminist framework to account for the lived experiences of black women. Race, gender, social status, and sexual orientation, among many other factors, were identified as operating in a complex way to produce discrimination. At present, the proximity between intersectionality, ecofeminism, and different interactionist practices has been highlighted. As A.E. Kings, among other scholars, has recently argued, "Intersectionality has helped to develop the practical application of ecofeminism by 'initiating a process of discovery (Davis 2008, p. 7), by acting as an analytical tool or 'lens' to aid critical thinking on ecofeminist debates". The place of good ecofeminist theory is not necessarily to provide ultimate answers but rather to allow for critical engagement with the multitude of experiences contributing to the discrimination of women and the environment, while at the same time recognizing the limitations and constraints of one's analysis" (Kings 2017, pp. 69–70).
[4] See Barad (2007, 2008) and Bennett (2010).

is distributed in an outright different manner across the world (Butler 2004, p. 24). In Butler's theorization, our lives are dependent on others (Butler 2004, p. 23), resulting in a condition of "primary vulnerability" (Butler 2004, p. 24). Each and every one of us depends on the decisions of others: in a most pressing way, our bodies are "given over" to others to be taken care of, and our bodies are "always something more than, and other than, ourselves" (Butler 2004, p. 25). In one of her examples, the many losses of lives to AIDS in Africa are compounded by their silencing in the media and by the absence of discursive elaborations on the meaning of these losses for their communities (Butler 2004, [p. 25]). These are but examples of how our existence is ruled by interrelationships, and of how it is these relationships, or lack thereof, which determine the livability of our lives. As Butler points out, on the basis of geographic and social considerations, the limits of what is knowable (Butler 2004, p. 27) or grievable (Butler 2004, p. 19) determine "radically different ways in which ... vulnerability is distributed throughout the globe" (Butler 2004, p. 24).[5]

Along the lines of current studies of vulnerability, Stacy Alaimo proposes the concept of "trans-corporeality" (Alaimo 2009, p. 25). She argues for the "recognition of the substantial interconnections between human corporeality and the more-than-human world," and defines vulnerability as "a sense of precarious, corporeal openness to the material world" (Alaimo 2009, p. 23). In her view, clearly, a pre-condition for the acknowledgement of vulnerability lies in the recognition of differences which compel us to expand our notion of what should be respected and protected, both ethically and within the law. In this sense, human and non-human ecological vulnerabilities should find an equal status in the larger picture of dynamic existence.

Alaimo and Susan Hekman hold that "Nature is agentic—it acts, and those actions have consequences for both the human and nonhuman world" (Alaimo and Hekman 2008, p. 5). They also acknowledge the new political dimension that both the human and the non-human acquire in the light of new materialist feminisms. Along this line, Tuana (2008) has studied Hurricane Katrina as an example to illustrate the many contending forces at play which make it, simultaneously, a natural and a social phenomenon. Her analysis includes "levees, the Army Corp of Engineers, global warming, the hurricane, the local politics of New Orleans, shell middens, the federal government, racial politics, and the poor and disabled populations of New Orleans" (Alaimo and Hekman 2008, p. 13). Tuana demonstrates how our former clear boundaries separating nature and culture, and human and non-human, are no longer epistemologically valid.

When it comes to vulnerability, at present, it is inevitable to pay attention to climate change. Chris Cuomo refers to the huge impact that anthropogenic climate change is having on life and to the different historical conditions of exploitation that different areas, populations, and communities have endured ever since colonial power and capitalism unleashed the terribly unbalanced situation we have now: "Climate change was manufactured in a crucible of inequality, for it is a product of the industrial and fossil-fuel eras, historical forces powered by exploitation, colonialism, and nearly limitless instrumental use of 'nature'" (Cuomo 2011, p. 693). For Cuomo, we are all at risk, "including those who have contributed little or nothing at all to the industrial greenhouse effect" (Cuomo 2011, p. 693).

In any event, it is precisely from the strength and creativity of social movements that a resistance to prevailing discourses of victimization is surfacing:

> ... from indigenous, anti-globalization, feminist, and youth movements for climate justice. These movements point out that many communities are in vulnerable positions precisely because they uphold ecological values that have not been engulfed by global capitalism and

---

[5] Butler has been critiqued for her excessive emphasis on discourse as the major force giving shape to human life. In parallel, Butler forgets to give a space to the non-human in her theorization, although she is well aware of the limits of humanism (Butler 2004, pp. 13, 35). The debate on "postmodern feminism['s] retreat from the material" (Alaimo and Hekman 2008, p. 3) is addressed by Colebrook (2008), Hekman (2008), Kirkby (2008), and Alaimo (2008). Along this line, further critiques can be found in Barad (2007), especially pp. 61–64.

technological modernization, recognizing marginal status in fossil-fuel cultures to be a sign
of wisdom and resilience rather than weakness. (Cuomo 2011, p. 695)

Stacy Alaimo too, argues that gender violence, limited access to resources, and rent imbalance has deeply affected women. As major actors of social change and coalition-building, "Feminist organizations such as Women's Environment and Development Organization (WEDO) are careful to complement feminine vulnerability with feminist agency, savvy, and survival strategies, calling for more parity in decision making and leadership" (Alaimo 2009, p. 312). The emphasis on parity and political representation, as much as women's progress in debunking the epistemological divide in the binary between nature and culture has brought about a paradigm shift in human positionings facing the world at large, human/non-human interaction, and living matter intra-actions. In Tuana's view, the current field of interactionism ushers us into "a world of complex phenomena in dynamic relationality" (Tuana 2008, p. 191). Environmentalists, green activists, and agro-ecological organizations have explored possibilities for alternative models for rural life. As I will attempt to show, in a domain as important as agriculture (which involves feeding the world, maintaining the biosphere, and preserving biodiversity), movements such as La Via Campesina support the livelihood of farmers by advocating an ethics of care with the land, protecting the rights of local and indigenous communities.

4. La Via Campesina: New Feminist Alternatives for the Environment

La Via Campesina (peasant popular feminism) is a feminist movement which grew out of the Movimento dos Trabalhadores Rurais Sem-Terra (MST) (Peasants without Land), where women identified the contradictions of the masculinized matrix based upon establishing large agrarian cooperatives that competed against big landowners, which proved to be unviable. Striving to reach food sovereignty for the people, feminists proposed to fight the huge agro-businesses in support of a sustainable and organic agriculture. Theirs is a combination of feminism and struggle against capital focusing on the fight against transnational corporations.

As Alaimo claims, we must take activism and other 'low' practices seriously "as inventive modes of political contestation" (Alaimo 2016, p. 13). In the La Via Campesina movement, a range of transformative micro-practices are present. Their practices—sit-ins, demonstrations, and performances—go well beyond the status quo in agriculture, land use, and food sovereignty (humans are certainly 'affected' by the land throughout their material and discursive practices). Among those practices, I will particularly discuss their resistance actions, their links to other voices of protest (Social and Food Justice), and their resistance to adopt genetically modified crops as major forms of raising awareness and gaining support for their cause.

From a new materialist perspective, peasant farming is respectful to the land with which it interacts by virtue of "intra-actions" (Barad 2007). For Barad, neither subjects nor objects exist outside of any particular practice, but rather, they are enacted in discrete intra-actions to which both human and non-human agencies contribute, affecting and becoming affected by their reciprocal operations. Subjects and objects are inseparably entangled, and indeterminacy is ever present in their associations. Barad's notion of matter entails a "stabilizing and de-stabilizing process" (Barad 2007, p. 151) and "'agent' in its ongoing materialization." In her account, "Agency is doing/being in its intra-activity" (Barad 2007, p. 235). Among those intra-actions, and crucially influential in the peasant's environment, the enhancement of biomass recycling and the optimization of the bioavailability of nutrients must be mentioned. From these intra-actions and proper soil management, peasants will end up increasing soil cover, maintaining diversity (humans do belong as another species within such diversity), and enhancing synergies with all the elements which share these ecosystems. Crucial for any approach to the work of La Via Campesina is the notion of indigenous knowledge[6] (which involves being

---

[6] Walter Mignolo has derived an important theoretical concept from Latin American intellectual Anibal Quijano when he speaks of the "coloniality of knowledge." This crucial idea is based on the erasure that colonial societies systematically

respectful to the land and its creatures), building inter-species and cross-cultural alliances, countering transnational corporations' land-grabbing (in Africa, Asia, and the Global South), alerting local communities (cross-sectionally) of risk, and securing resources for women and the dispossessed which are respectful to the land. Nancy Tuana's "interactionist ontology of viscous porosity" (in Alaimo 2008) in her commitment to take seriously the agency of the natural acts as an important paradigm for the comments and ideas that follow. In any event, it is the reciprocal insight of Western academia and indigenous philosophies and epistemologies that one should always acknowledge because the "appropriation of indigenous thinking in European contexts without indigenous interlocutors present to hold the use of indigenous stories and laws to account flattens, distorts and erases the embodied, legal-governance and spiritual aspects of Indigenous thinking" (Todd 2016, p. 9). In other words, the ongoing colonial imperatives of the academy must be a continued matter of concern and elicit a responsible engagement as a crucial element in the ethics of research.

In an effort to avoid what Rob Nixon calls the pervasive "slow violence" always present in the "environmentalism of the poor" (in Alaimo 2016, p. 175), La Via Campesina embodies a holistic approach in which there are no detached objects or elements but rather a series of intra-actions among the different realities to be considered. Along these lines, thinking through the relations between individuals and ecosystems seems to be where current research in environmental, social sciences, and feminist thinking is leading. Embodied in the feminist relations to the environment have always been the material and political practices that women have pursued with strategy and tactics. The traditional feminist ethics of care have opened up towards a more comprehensive, global ethics for all "matters of care" (see Puig de la Bellacasa 2017 and below).

Beginning in the 1990s, La Via Campesina has successfully gathered organizations of peasants, farmers, farm workers, and indigenous agrarian communities from across the globe. Its major endeavor has been to build collaborations and cooperation among its membership using various strategies and mechanisms that intersect at the local, regional, national, and international levels. The movement's progressive work on questions of gender inequality and hemispheric and regional differences is a crucial part of its objective of building community and coalition work.[7]

Traditionally, rural women have played a major role in agricultural production and in maintaining the social and economic fabric of their communities. Yet, it is a fact these women still have limited access to policy planning and decision making. In many cases, they continue to be excluded from political power positions, and, consequently, of major involvement in strategic planning and in all issues related to the quality of life of farming communities. Thus, when it comes to gender, with the pressing issues that affect women's economies and lives, La Via Campesina's women took action and got organized. In the Managua Declaration of 1992, women farmers were mentioned only once. In any event, from then onwards there was an increasing visibility of women farm leaders who made up 20% of the participants. It is important to note that at this meeting an effort was made to integrate indigenous peasant organizations, whose goals included to analyze and understand the challenges faced by indigenous peasant women. The worldwide struggle of indigenous organizations for ownership and control over productive resources is absolutely central in how La Via Campesina tackles the questions of ethnicity and contributes to their struggles. Almost from the start, La Via Campesina aimed to integrate both peasant and indigenous identities, since their approaches to the land, the earth, and territory, and their ideas regarding agriculture were substantially different.

Progressively gender concerns have been foregrounded, and ever since the 1993 "Framework for Action", the role that women and youth play in rural organizations has been recognized. Building

---

perform of indigenous forms of knowledge and their physical forms of transmission. As he writes, "[T]he word *epistemology* was used to disavow epistemological practices that did not correspond to the Western management of knowledge" (Mignolo 2011, p. 172).

[7] For an interesting and well-documented account on La Via Campesina, which has informed my thinking on this movement, see the important book by Annette A. Desmarais (2007).

leadership capacity among women farm leaders counts among their foremost priorities. Women have also strongly contributed to further define La Via Campesina's position on food sovereignty, which includes: (a) favoring organic production, (b) reducing the use of potentially harmful fertilizers, and (c) initiating an immediate halt to the trade of banned agrochemicals (Desmarais 2003, p. 143). After these early discussions, it became clear that no food sovereignty would be achieved without the strong involvement of women in policy development in the different communities (Desmarais 2003, p. 143).

From 1996 to 2000, La Via Campesina Women's Commission concentrated its work in the Americas in its three major regions: Central America, South America, and the Caribbean. In their discussions, crucial issues such as human rights, struggles for agrarian reform, management of natural resources, biodiversity, and the impact of agricultural trade were considered central for food sovereignty. This period was a turning point in raising awareness of the importance of women working on equal terms with their male counterparts to build an alternative agricultural model. At the third International Via Campesina Conference, a "Via Campesina Gender Position Paper" was approved, placing women and gender issues at the heart of the movement; " ... [I]t is fitting and necessary to articulate a gender analysis in order to shape inclusive, just and viable long-term solutions." (Via Campesina Third International Conference, quoted in Desmarais 2007, p. 176). This document elaborated on three main principles: equality and human rights, economic justice, and social development, with "each clearly specifying the role, needs and interests of women" (Desmarais 2003, p. 144); it has been of major importance and has produced a balancing effect in the responsibilities of all actors implicated in the preservation of life on the planet. At this stage in the Anthropocene and in the consideration of women's roles, labor, and social expectations placed on them, new materialist insights into an ethics of care which transcends the human, and, thus, sexual difference, are certainly liberatory for humanity as a whole, and for the environment. As Puig de la Bellacasa insists on " ... the moral undertones that invite us to transcend the 'human' for something 'more than.' It also starts from a human center, then to reach 'beyond.'" (Puig de la Bellacasa 2017, p. 2). What we cannot ignore is the fact that,

> Care is a human trouble, but this does not make care a human-only matter. Affirming the absurdity of disentangling human and nonhuman relations of care and the ethicalities involved requires decentering human agencies, as well as remining close to the predicaments and inheritances of situated human doings. (Puig de la Bellacasa 2017, p. 2)

Since its inception, La Via Campesina has opposed the introduction of genetically modified crops into worldwide agricultural systems. While recognizing their potential to alleviate shortages in food production, the organization considers that the dangers associated with their use outweigh any beneficial effect. Apart from any future unknown or unforeseen consequences of the use of genetically modified crops, La Via Campesina sees two immediate problems associated with their use. First is their control by large transnational corporations and second is their negative effects on biodiversity. Regarding large corporations, the development and marketing of genetically modified crops is aggressively promoted by large transnational agribusiness corporations (exemplified by Monsanto) that impose stringent control over the seeds and that require the extensive use of agrotoxics of their own manufacture, thus closing a circle where farmers are absolutely dependent on these transnational companies. This tight control of crop markets by large agribusiness corporations is becoming even more stringent with a recent wave of fusions into mega corporations within the agribusiness market. As part of this wave, Dow Chemicals fused with DuPont, Monsanto was acquired by Bayer AG, and Syngenta partnered with ChemChina. An immediate result of this oligopoly is the ensuing lack of food security for regions where farmers are unable to pay the prices that these corporations establish. Regarding biodiversity, the negative impact of genetically modified crops is two-fold. On one hand, the use of just a few varieties of common crops poses the risk of losing the necessary biodiversity of these crops in the form of less-used varieties as a source of genetic material for the development of new varieties in the future. On the other hand, the increased use of agrotoxics associated with genetically modified crops determines a high risk of eliminating a large part of the non-crop biodiversity in the planet.

5. La Via Campesina: Insurgent Practices

La Via Campesina opposes the uncontrolled entry of foreign capital into local agricultural and food production. Apart from resulting in an impoverishment of farmers, given that large corporations use their economic might to impose their harsh market conditions on farmers, these corporations are a source of food insecurity for local communities, as food production, rather than being guaranteed, is subject to the vagaries of the markets. A well-known example is that of the fight that MST, an active Brazilian member of La Via Campesina, has been undertaking against transnational corporations in Brazil.

5.1. Cevasa's Occupation: Against Agribusiness

On 9 March 2007, over nine hundred women occupied the Cevasa sugar mill and power plant, located in the region of Ribeirão Preto, São Paulo state. This action was widely covered in the news and has later been reviewed by Abramsky (2010). The previous year, a major part (63%) of the shares of Cevasa were bought by Cargill, a large American global corporation in the food, agriculture, and industrial markets, and the world's largest privately held corporation in terms of revenue (Bodley 2012, p. 205).

Cevasa's was the largest sugarcane mill in Brazil: it produced 1.4 million tons of cane sugar per year or 125,000 L of alcohol. After Cargill bought a large part of the Cevasa plant, the previous owners used the money to buy another mill in the Western state of Acre. This practice of selling part of the capital of local mills to foreign companies with the subsequent expansion of production in other regions of Brazil and Latin America is common in Ribeirão Preto and contributes to an ongoing de-localization of agricultural production.

During their action, La Via Campesina women defended the adoption of an alternative agricultural model which privileges the small farmer (responsible for the production of a good part of the food crops) and that implements an agrarian reform that modifies the land structure of the country. The region of Ribeirão Preto was chosen for this action because it symbolizes the expansion of sugarcane estates, a model based on the overexploitation of peasants (more than 15 workers there have died of exhaustion in the past three years), and the destruction of the environment.

The occupation was part of La Via Campesina's action "Women in Defence of Life and Against Agribusiness". Through this, rural workers undertook to denounce the false promises of agribusiness in relation to sugarcane planting and to ethanol production, alerting people to the real consequences of increased sugarcane cultivation for the environment, the pollution of fires and the respiratory diseases caused by them, the vast extent of land concentration in Brazil, and the consequent increase in social differences.[8]

This action was linked to a large demonstration against the state visit of American president George W. Bush to Brazil. President Bush had been very interested in the promotion of bioalcohol as a fuel for automation because it provided a convenient outlet for the U.S.' large stocks of surplus grains. Following that, major American firms became interested in the production of bioethanol at low cost, and his visit was interpreted as an attempt to negotiate with then Brazilian president Lula da Silva access to Brazilian sugarcane bioalcohol. For MST, bioethanol is not a clean energy but an environmentally damaging one that in addition only serves to convert Brazil into "the backyard of the American elites."

---

[8] Subsequently, sugarcane field burning, a traditional practice, has been banned in the state of São Paulo, a legislation that these protests helped implement (São-Paulo-Environmental-System 2017).

The way the Cevasa occupation unfolded demonstrates how La Via Campesina stages its actions. The occupation by women took place peacefully and no goods were damaged. Not wanting to risk the onset of violence between demonstrators and employees, after being assured that no damage would be caused to the facilities, the plant's directors gave license to workers of the daily shift.

5.2. Nestlé: Predatory Exploitation of Water Resources

Also in Brazil, on 20 March 2018, the MST movement staged an occupation of a Nestlé mineral water processing factory in São Lourenço, state of Minas Gerais. As it was reported (EFE 2018), again, very early in the morning, a group of six hundred women from the MST occupied the plant protesting the privatization of water, which, they claimed, was going to be traded in the 8th World Water Forum to be held in Brasilia. In their denunciation, the MST accused then president Michel Temer of selling their water to international corporations.

The MST accused the Forum of being just a marketplace for negotiations with high executives from companies such as Nestlé and Coca-Cola for the exploitation of Brazil's water resources. The MST cited Nestlé as an example of a transnational corporation established in Brazil for decades undertaking predatory and irregular forms of natural resources exploitation. For the MST water is a common good of humanity and defending it is a matter of sovereignty. The MST further denounced that in January 2018, President Temer and Nestlé President Paul Bulcke met to discuss the exploitation of the Guarani Aquifer, a massive reserve that covers four countries (Brazil, Argentina, Paraguay, and Uruguay). The Nestlé company, which controls 10.5% of the world's water market, has been installed in Minas Gerais since 1994, when it bought the sources and the Parque das Águas de São Lourenço. Since 1997, the local population has denounced the exploitation of mineral waters that were widely used for medicinal treatments before being privatized. Besides the reduction in the available water flow, the MST denounced changes in taste of the water due to over-exploitation. These allegations have been dismissed by the Nestlé company, which accused in turn the MST of causing damage to their São Lourenço plant facilities.

5.3. Punta de Agua: Countering Land-Grabbing

One of the aims of La Via Campesina is to help farmers, who are often associated with native minorities, fight against land-grabbing by large agroindustrial corporations or even by local authorities, who are usually acting on behalf of hidden economic interests. In land-grabbing, an established pattern emerges. Farmer families, who have worked their land for generations, are confronted by large agribusiness who take advantage of the fact that these families seldom register their lands to inscribe them in their name. They then exhibit titles of ownership of the farmers' lands and try to expel them. This is a dramatic matter of concern for La Via Campesina's activism. As Puig de la Bellacasa has argued, "Soils are now up on the list of environmental matters calling for global care [...] [soils] are a new frontier for knowledge and fascination about the life teaming [sic] in this dark alterity. Human persistent mistreatment and neglect of soils is emphasized in calls that connect the economic, political and ethical value of soils to matters of human survival" (Puig de la Bellacasa 2017, p. 169).

La Via Campesina organizes actions to resist these evictions and to force authorities to recognize ancestral ownership rights for farmers. A case in point took place in June 2016 at Punta de Agua, in San Rafael, Mendoza, Argentina (Unión de Trabajadores Sin Tierra-Movimiento Nacional Campesino Indígena (UST-MNCI) 2016). There, mapuche farmers who have lived off their land for generations were ordered to vacate their land by legal representatives of the transnational company Laguna Blue-Agua Segura, who exhibited titles of ownership, trespassed their fences, threatened them, and used physical force trying to expel them. The La Via Campesina-affiliated UST-MNCI movement immediately mobilized its members to counteract these actions. Some years back, the same company, claiming property rights, had fenced off the Punto de Agua village, effectively isolating 300 families on the basis of claimed property rights of land surrounding the settlement. Mobilizations of UST-MNCI had then forced the company to remove the fences.

Following the June 2016 threats, UST-MNCI mobilized their members in the region, including women and men, who demonstrated in Punta de Agua and publicly denounced these actions. On 27 June 2016, UST-MNCI activists blocked streets in Punta de Agua and in the presence of San Rafael municipal workers and two members of parliament demanded that authorities recognize ownership of traditionally farmed land and block new registrations of previously unclaimed lands. They further demanded the presence of authorities to enforce removal of wire fences in community land now claimed by the transnational corporation, stating that inaction on the part of authorities would be answered by "farmer's justice" and forceful removal of these fences. After this action, attempts of the corporation to reclaim farmers' lands continued. Finally, in light of the UST-MNCI resistance, in August 2016, local authorities annulled newly issued property rights and recognized ownership of the land by the mapuche families who had traditionally farmed it. As activist Paula Gioia remarks, "The land where our cattle grazes, where we produce our hay, where we grow cereals and vegetables, the forests from where we make our heating wood and the water sources for our drinking and for irrigation can not been handled as commodities!" (La_Via_Campesina (@via_campesina) 2018).

With the kind of activist protests I have described, La Via Campesina has come to represent in many ways the entanglements that for Karen Barad redefine the human in light of its connectivity with non-human others and "the relationalities of becoming of which we are a part" (Barad 2007, p. 393). Recognition of such entanglements, in other words, shifts the focus "from unitary to nomadic subjectivity" (Braidotti 2013, p. 49). Barad's understanding of connectivity and relationality eschews unitariness and self-centeredness and leads in the direction of Braidotti's views on nomadic subjectivity. This "nomadism" emerges when the subject resists being fixed within a rigid frame constricting its movement and expansion:

> Though the image of "nomadic subjects" is inspired by the experience of peoples or cultures that are literally nomadic, the nomadism in question here refers to the kind of critical consciousness that resists settling into socially coded modes of thought and behaviour. Not all nomads are world travelers; some of the greatest trips can take place without physically moving from one's habitat. It is the subversion of set conventions that defines the nomadic state, not the literal act of traveling. (Braidotti 2011, p. 5)

Acknowledging that the human is embedded within a large network of other social, biological, political, semiotic and other forces opens up a trans-species network where non-human others are recognized as co-participants and bearers of agency and accountability. These non-human others include other biological entities such as water, soils, geological layers, seeds, bio-fertilizers, and a long list of elements whose contribution to life as we know it in the planet would be unthinkable. As I have attempted to show, the intra-actions among deeply connected environmental and social issues have become an inexhaustible source of "transgressed boundaries, potent fusions, and dangerous possibilities [...] as one part of needed political work" (Haraway 1991, p. 154). As Mozambican activist Graça Samo, International Coordinator of the World March of Women, reminding us of the importance of ancestors for indigenous populations, asserts, "The moment in which we are living now is a time of extremes ... This has to be something that makes us as a global feminist movement to come together and say, what is our strategy in this moment? What is the right way to position ourselves to take control of the political struggle? [...] We are not inventing, we are reclaiming the forms that our ancestors have been using" (Samo 2019).

6. Concluding Remarks: Re-Distributing, Re-Thinking, Responding to the Planet

Prompted by Jacques Derrida's philosophical considerations on his visual interaction with his cat (Derrida 2002) and by Barbara Smuts' baboon ethology studies (Smuts 1985.), Donna Haraway has argued that, as it is with humans, interacting with non-humans is not simply about reacting to them, but rather about establishing a bidirectional communication (Haraway 2008, pp. 19–27), about "looking back," (Haraway 2008, p. 106), and about accepting that one can establish communication in a reciprocal way.

As I have attempted to show, it is imperative that an engaged involvement with the current status of the degradation of the planet at this stage of late capitalism gains momentum. Through grassroots activist actions, organized protest, and strategic communication, social movements urge us to move towards an ethics of care, protection, and respect for the planet. It is only by means of a cultural and educational awareness, deeply inspired by the teachings of new materialist philosophies, deep ecology, practices of re-distribution of resources, and social justice initiatives, that current practices of labor, consumption, and development can make progress and bring about significant changes in the relations of all elements and actors at play.

When it comes to the shibboleth of "sustainability", philosopher Val Plumwood has argued that "[t]he often-invoked term 'sustainability' tends to obscure the seriousness of the situation [of ecological crisis]; clearly no culture which sets in motion massive processes of biospheric degradation which it has normalized, and which it cannot respond or correct can hope to survive for very long" (Plumwood 2002, p. 1). Along the same lines, Benson and Craig have argued that sustainability might no longer be an appropriate course of action under current conditions, given that "'sustainability' refers to the long term ability to continue to engage in a particular activity," and "assumes that we (a) know what can be sustained and (b) have the capacity to maintain stationarity," (Benson and Craig 2014, p. 107). For them, "with climate change, we face a future in which we have no idea what we can sustain" (2014, p. 107), a future where "resiliency" is more likely to succeed than sustainability because "resilience thinking acknowledges disequilibrium and nonlinear, continual change—often as a result of crossing a 'tipping point' or threshold [...] and reorients us to focus on coping with change" (2014, p. 107). Coping with change, recovering quickly from difficulties, and being "resilient" also implies being able to redefine our interactions with an environment subject to critical modifications. Would it be possible—indeed, one cannot not acknowledge the possibility—for (multi)species relationships "to avoid commensalism or parasitism while yet occurring inside differential relations of power? [...] Mutualism is not so much about equality as reciprocity across difference" (Garvey 2014, p. 143). According to Canadian *métis* anthropologist Zoe Todd, "[T]he climate, Sila, is an incredibly important organizing concept for many actors in Inuit territories [...] Sila is both climate and a life force" (Todd 2016, p. 6). Todd denounces the absence in Western academia of indigenous voices who are strongly engaged in crucial issues for the survival of the planet, such as climate change. Millie Thrasher, Rosemarie Kuptana, and climate change activist Sheila Watt-Cloutier (who was nominated for the Nobel Peace Prize alongside Al Gore in 2007) deserve a special mention for their sustained activism and scholarly work on many fronts. Todd raises the poignant question of when Euro-American scholarship will take the intellectual labor and activist work of Inuit women seriously (Todd 2016, p. 7).

Revisiting Donna Haraway's recent ideas in *Staying with the Trouble* (Haraway 2016), she elaborates on the symbiotic entanglements within the natural world in the direction of creating a multispecies ethic of "living-with": "Living with and dying with each other potently in the Chthulucene can be a fierce reply to the dictates of both Anthropos and Capital" (Haraway 2016, p. 2). Nonetheless, Haraway's caveat should also be addressed; in her view, "*Symbiosis* [*living with*, my emphasis] is not a synonym for mutually beneficial" (Haraway 2016, p. 60), and *sympoiesis* (her coinage), entails "'making with.' Nothing makes itself; nothing is really autopoietic or self-organizing" (Haraway 2016, p. 58). Haraway's "with-ness" helps us respond and become "respondents" to the inequalities and differences populating our planet, integrating material practices and situated knowledges. Staying with the trouble implies learning to coexist respectfully with the world of matter. Environmental geographer Juanita Sundberg states that "indigenous authors in the Americas [...] outline complex knowledge systems in which animals, plants and spirits are understood as beings who participate in the everyday practices that bring worlds into being. These epistemic traditions are not organized in and through dualist ontologies of nature/culture" (Sundberg 2013, p. 35). Along these lines, Sami political scientist Rauna Kuokkanen differentiates between learning to know the other and learning as an engagement with the other, and calls for learning as "participatory reciprocity", i.e., being attentive to other epistemes (indigenous, black, ...) as part of the geopolitical present (Kuokkanen 2007, p. 118; quoted. in Sundberg 2013, p. 40).

It is precisely at this point where a feminist, new materialist, and environmental-justice-informed activism can have a larger impact: though humanity and the practices of extractive capitalism[9] have profoundly transformed and damaged life in the planet for years to come, a new generation of green activists can claim redress and gain visibility and political representation for a new reparative agenda. In the face of this bleak panorama, there remain submerged perspectives and other modes of perception that see, hear, and imagine life-worlds that escape the current corporate, extractive impulse. Indigenous epistemologies, grassroots ecological initiatives, and transnational protest movements should probably join forces in this common endeavor to save the planet. It is in the creation of emergent spaces through collective action, politics, writing, art, and community building that an engaged humanity can strive to counter destruction and death. Only at this stage can we expect to remedy the ills of overexploitation, exhaustion, and ravaging the resources of the Earth in our endeavor to remain cohabitants of the planet.

Funding: This research received no external funding.

Conflicts of Interest: The author declares no conflict of interest.

References

Abramsky, Kolia. 2010. Some Brief News Reports from Direct Action-based Resistance from Around the World: Brazil, UK, Germany and the Philippines. In *Sparking a Worlwide Energy Revolution: Social Struggles in the Transition to a Post-Petrol World*. Edited by Kolia Abramsky. Oakland: AK Press, pp. 482–84.

Alaimo, Stacy. 2000. *Undomesticated Ground: Recasting Nature as a Feminist Space*. Ithaca: Cornell University Press.

Alaimo, Stacy. 2008. Trans-Corporeal Feminisms and the Ethical Space of Nature. In *Material Feminisms*. Edited by Stacy Alaimo and Susan Hekman. Bloomington: Indiana University Press, pp. 237–64.

Alaimo, Stacy. 2009. Insurgent Vulnerability and the Carbon Footprint of Gender. *Women, Gender, and Research (Kinder, Kon, og Forskning, Denmark)* 3: 22–35. [CrossRef]

Alaimo, Stacy. 2016. *Exposed: Environmental Politics and Pleasures in Posthuman Times*. Minneapolis: University of Minnesota Press.

Alaimo, Stacy, and Susan H. Hekman. 2008. Emerging Models of Materiality in Feminist Theory. In *Material Feminisms*. Edited by Stacy Alaimo and Susan Hekman. Bloomington: Indiana University Press, pp. 1–19.

Barad, Karen. 2007. *Meeting the Universe Halfway: Quantum Physics and the Entanglement of Matter and Meaning*. Durham: Duke University Press.

Barad, Karen. 2008. Posthumanist Performativity: Toward an Understanding of How Matter Comes to Matter. In *Material Feminisms*. Edited by Stacy Alaimo and Susan Hekman. Bloomington: Indiana University Press, pp. 120–54.

Barrett, Estelle, Nathalie Blanc, Olga Cielemecka, Felicity Colman, Rick Dolphijn, Ilona Hongisto, Kaisa Kontturi, Thomas Lamarche, Thea Manola, Frédéric Neyrat, and et al. 2017. Paris Conference on Environmental Humanities and New Materialisms. Available online: https://pariscostconf.sciencesconf.org/data/pages/NewMat_Programme_Interactif.pdf (accessed on 10 March 2019).

Bennett, Jane. 2010. *Vibrant Matter: A Political Ecology of Things*. Durham: Duke University Press.

Benson, Melinda H., and Robin K. Craig. 2014. The End of Sustainability: The Realities of the Anthropocene Demand a New Approach to Environmental Governance. *Ensia*. July 8. Available online: http://ensia.com/voices/the-end-of-sustainability/ (accessed on 10 March 2019).

Blaser, Mario. 2009. The Threat of the Yrmo: The Political Ontology of a Sustainable Hunting Program. *American Anthropologist* 111: 10–20. [CrossRef]

---

[9] See Gómez-Barris' important *The Extractive Zone: Social Ecologies and Decolonial Perspectives* (Gómez-Barris 2017). Here, the author analyses the oppositional practices that have forcefully emerged in different locations against extractive capitalism, including not only the intellectual and theoretical basis of these resistances, but also the work of artists and activists in response to those exploitative and abusive practices.

Blaser, Mario. 2012. Ontology and Indigeneity: On the Political Ontology of Heterogeneous Assemblages. *Cultural Geographies* 21: 49–58. [CrossRef]

Bodley, John H. 2012. *Anthropology and Contemporary Human Problems*, 6th ed. Lanham: Altamira Press.

Braidotti, Rosi. 2011. *Nomadic Subjects: Embodiment and Sexual Difference in Contemporary Feminist Theory*. New York: Columbia University Press.

Braidotti, Rosi. 2013. *The Posthuman*. Cambridge: Polity Press.

Butler, Judith. 2004. *Undoing Gender*. New York: Routledge.

Colebrook, Claire. 2008. On Not Becoming Man: The Materialist Politics of Unactualized Potential. In *Material Feminisms*. Edited by Stacy Alaimo and Susan Hekman. Bloomington: Indiana University Press, pp. 52–84.

Colebrook, Claire. 2017. We Have Always Been Post-Anthropocene: The Anthropocene Counterfactual. In *Anthropocene Feminism*. Edited by Richard Grusin. Minneapolis: University of Minnesota Press, pp. 1–20.

Cuomo, Chris. 2011. Climate Change, Vulnerability, and Responsibility. *Hypatia* 26: 690–714. [CrossRef]

Crenshaw, Kimberlé. 1989. Demarginalizing the Intersection of Race and Sex: A Black Feminist Critique of Antidiscrimination Doctrine. *The University of Chicago Legal Forum* 1989: 139–67.

Derrida, Jacques. 2002. The Animal That Therefore I Am (More to Follow). *Critical Inquiry* 28: 369–418. [CrossRef]

Desmarais, Annette A. 2003. The Via Campesina: Peasant Women at the Frontiers of Food Sovereignty. *Canadian Woman Studies/Les cahiers de la femme* 23: 140–45.

Desmarais, Annette A. 2007. *La Via Campesina: Globalization and the Power of Peasants*. London: Pluto Press.

EFE. 2018. MST Ocupa Fábrica da Nestlé em MG e diz Que Governo Negocia Água Brasileira. Available online: https://www.efe.com/efe/brasil/brasil/mst-ocupa-fabrica-da-nestle-em-mg-e-diz-que-governo-negocia-agua-brasileira/50000239-3559336 (accessed on 10 March 2019).

Garvey, Michelle Jenneman. 2014. Restoration's Return in the Age of Climate Crisis: Toward a Feminist Environmental Justice Response. Ph.D. dissertation, University of Minnesota, Minneapolis, MN, USA. Available online: https://conservancy.umn.edu/bitstream/handle/11299/171098/Garvey_umn_0130E_15590.pdf (accessed on 10 March 2019).

Gómez-Barris, Macarena. 2017. *The Extractive Zone: Social Ecologies and Decolonial Perspectives*. Durham: Duke University Press.

Haraway, Donna J. 1991. *Simians, Cyborgs, and Women: The Reinvention of Nature*. New York and London: Routledge.

Haraway, Donna J. 1997. *Modest_Witness@Second_Millennium.Female_Man©_Meets_Oncomouse™: Feminism and Technoscience*. New York and London: Routledge.

Haraway, Donna J. 2008. *When Species Meet*. Minneapolis: University of Minnesota Press.

Haraway, Donna J. 2016. *Staying with the Trouble: Making Kin in the Chthulucene*. Durham: Duke University Press.

Hekman, Susan. 2008. Constructing the Ballast: An Ontology for Feminism. In *Material Feminisms*. Edited by Stacy Alaimo and Susan Hekman. Bloomington: Indiana University Press, pp. 85–119.

Kohn, Eduardo. 2013. *How Forests Think: Towards an Anthropology Beyond the Human*. Berkeley: University of California Press.

Kings, A. E. 2017. Intersectionality and the Changing Face of Ecofeminism. *Ethics & the Environment* 22: 63–87.

Kuokkanen, Rauna. 2007. *Reshaping the University: Responsibility, Indigenous Epistemes, and the Logic of the Gift*. Vancouver: University of British Columbia Press.

La_Via_Campesina (@via_campesina). 2018. Post. Twitter. April 10. Available online: https://twitter.com/via_campesina/status/983633026516041729 (accessed on 10 March 2019).

Martinez-Torres, María Elena, and Peter Rosset. 2010. La Via Campesina: The Birth and Evolution of a Transnational Social Movement. *Journal of Peasant Studies* 37: 149–75. [CrossRef]

Mignolo, Walter D. 2011. *The Darker Side of Western Modernity: Global Futures, Decolonial Options*. Durham: Duke University Press.

Plumwood, Val. 1993. *Feminism and the Mastery of Nature*. London: Routledge.

Plumwood, Val. 2002. *Environmental Culture: The Ecological Crisis of Reason*. London: Routledge.

Puig de la Bellacasa, Maria. 2017. *Matters of Care: Speculative Ethics in More Than Human Worlds*. Minneapolis: University of Minnesota Press.

Samo, Maria da Graça. 2019. War Abroad, War at Home: From Venezuela, Honduras, Haiti to Miami (3/20 Webinar). Available online: http://ggjalliance.org/Anti-WarWebinar (accessed on 14 July 2019).

São-Paulo-Environmental-System. 2017. Agro-Environmental Protocol Reduces in 90% Area of Sugarcane Burning in São Paulo. Available online: https://www.infraestruturameioambiente.sp.gov.br/en/2017/06/07/agro-environmental-protocol-reduces-in-90-area-of-sugarcane-burning-in-sao-paulo/ (accessed on 10 March 2019).

Shiva, Vandana. 1989. *Staying Alive: Women, Ecology and Development*. London: Zed Books.

Smuts, Barbara. 1985. *Sex and Friendship in Baboons*. Cambridge: Harvard University Press.

Sundberg, Juanita. 2013. Decolonizing Posthumanist Geographies. *Cultural Geographies* 21: 33–47. [CrossRef]

Tsing, Anna Lowenhaupt, Heather Anne Swanson, Elaine Gan, and Nils Bubandt, eds. 2017. *Arts of Living on a Damaged Planet: Ghosts and Monsters of the Anthropocene*. Minneapolis: University of Minnesota Press.

Todd, Zoe. 2016. An Indigenous Feminist's Take on the Ontological Turn: 'Ontology' Is Just Another Word for Colonialism. *Journal of Historical Sociology* 29: 4–22. [CrossRef]

Tuana, Nancy. 2008. Viscous Porosity: Witnessing Katrina. In *Material Feminisms*. Edited by Stacy Alaimo Susan Hekman. Bloomington: Indiana University Press, pp. 188–213.

UST-MNCI. 2016. Argentina, Mendoza, Corte de Calle y Asamblea Campesina y Popular en Punta del Agua: Por la Tierra y la Vida. Available online: https://www.farmlandgrab.org/26284 (accessed on 10 March 2019).

 © 2019 by the author. Licensee MDPI, Basel, Switzerland. This article is an open access article distributed under the terms and conditions of the Creative Commons Attribution (CC BY) license (http://creativecommons.org/licenses/by/4.0/).

Article

New Materialist Perspectives on Sex Robots. A Feminist Dystopia/Utopia?

Tanja Kubes

Gender Studies in Science and Engineering, Technical University of Munich, 80333 Munich, Germany; tanja.kubes@tum.de

Received: 30 April 2019; Accepted: 23 July 2019; Published: 26 July 2019

Abstract: Feminist discourses on sex robots and robot sex largely focus on the dystopian fear of an exponentiation of hegemonic masculinity. The very possibility of robot sex is put on a level with slavery or prostitution and is rejected as a continuation of male dominance over women. Proceeding from a feminist new materialist perspective and building both on the refutation of normative definitions of sex and a general openness to the manifold variants consenting adults can engage in in sexual matters, the article presents a queer alternative to this outright rejection. Leaving the beaten tracks of pornographic mimicry, sex robots may in fact enable new liberated forms of sexual pleasure beyond fixed normalizations, thus contributing to a sex-positive utopian future.

Keywords: new materialism; sex robots; robot sex; transversalism; human–machine interaction; sex-positive; diffractive design; queer studies

---

A popular topic in movies from Fritz Lang's *Metropolis* (1927) to Alex Garland's *Ex Machina* (2014) or Netflix' *Westworld* (2016), hyperfeminine humanoid robots have fueled the imagination of cinemagoers for almost a century. Today, however, for the first time in human history, lifelike humanoid robots serving as counterparts for romantic and sexual encounters are no longer just a fantasy of science fiction authors. Advances in the fields of artificial intelligence, biomechanics, robotics, and animatronics have them emerging on the horizon as a real possibility, causing a fundamental shift of the narrative from the imaginary to the tangible, from fiction to facticity. It does not come as a surprise, therefore, that over the past two or so years, sex robots have had their fair share of media coverage. New York Times (Bates 2017), Washington Post (Guarino 2018), CNN (Kerner 2018), Foxnews (Shaw 2018), ABC news (Sparrow 2019), Frankfurter Allgemeine Zeitung (FAZ 2018), Süddeutsche Zeitung (Weber 2018), BBC (Varley 2018), ARTE (Miethge 2017), ZEIT (Beschorner 2017), Focus (Schmieder 2019)—hardly any major newspaper, magazine, or TV station has managed to ignore the manifold efforts to construct intelligent machines that raise human–machine interaction to a whole new level. Most of the reports warned against the dangers of building humanoid robots or of introducing artificial intelligence in our bedrooms. The very possibility of an emotional closeness of humans and robots was dismissed as some technocrats' dystopian fantasy that we should prevent from becoming reality the sooner the better. Already back in 2015, British anthropologist Kathleen Richardson and robotics researcher Erik Billing launched the *Campaign Against Sex Robots* that has since drawn attention to the many ethical questions raised by the prospect of sexual encounters between humans and machines. Such problems do indeed exist. Prototypes of sex robots aiming to hit the market in the near future are definitely hinting towards a questionable understanding of ideals of female beauty and the nature of gender relations. In this context, one can also ask, why almost all sex robots currently developed are 'female.' There certainly is a market for robots beyond a heterosexist norm, however, the industry acts as if it were nonexistent.

Another problem commonly addressed by robot sex critics is that, by treating robots as objects, we run the risk of eventually objectifying humans in a similar way (Gee 2017; Richardson 2015). Richardson even goes one step further, equalling robot sex with slavery and prostitution (Richardson 2016). Consequently, there have been repeated calls for a complete ban. The reasons put forward are very similar to those of a feminist movement from the 1980s: the fight against pornography (e.g., Dworkin 1989; Morgan 1980). Also, just like in those earlier discussions, the feminist critique finds itself in the odd neighbourhood of anti-feminist conservatives arguing strongly in favour of restricted sexual morals. Starting from a queer perspective building both on the refutation of normative definitions of sex and a general openness to the manifold variants consenting adults can engage in in sexual matters, I shall present a feminist alternative to the outright rejection of sex robots and robot sex. While it may be true that current prototypes of sex robots address virtually exclusively heterosexual male customers, I argue that this does not necessarily oblige feminists to discard the very idea of robot sex altogether. On the contrary, allowing for the general possibility of robot sex, feminists can seize the opportunity to reclaim agency in the arena of human–machine interaction and try to change it in order to satisfy a larger variety of sexual tastes and thus increase the general "coefficient of transversality" (Bosteels 1998, p. 157). Here too, obviously, the argument somewhat resembles earlier—sex-positive feminist—responses to the anti-pornography movement of the 1970s and 1980s (e.g., Rubin 1984).

Proceeding from a new materialist perspective, I will then propose a reconsideration of design options for sex robots. The idea is actually quite simple: Instead of buttressing gender stereotypes and perpetuating a discourse of male domination by silicone means, the industry might as well explore the emancipatory potential held by intelligent machines acting as (virtually) equal counterparts in *all* types of social interaction. However, this thought does not seem to come natural to many engineers. It has to be promoted. Refusing dialogue with the people who actually develop sex robots, therefore, is a bad idea, if we hope to counter the possible negative effects of humanoid robots on society and try to deploy them for an entirely different purpose: to deconstruct gender stereotypes, to liberate humanism from its anthropocentric limitations, and to redefine our entanglement with the realm of the nonhuman in terms of a diffractive "ethico-onto-epistem-ology" (Barraclough 2018).

Feminist new materialism, object-oriented ontology (OOO), and actor network theory (ANT) provide the theoretical backdrop against which I will develop my argument. All three confront the tacit ontologism of our scientific renderings of the world and focus on both the capacity of things/objects to *act* and the irreducible eventfulness of matter. In this context, the human body as the most obvious factor of being in the world has received renewed interest (Rogowska-Stangret 2017). It is perceived as neither a simple *effect* of semantic attributions nor as the mere result of discursive practices. Semiotics (e.g., Eco 1987) and social constructivism (Butler 1990) may roughly delineate the field of 'making sense' of the world. However, new materialism has elevated matter (animate and inanimate) from its passive role and apprehended it as an *actant* (Latour 2002a), actively contributing to the very process of its materialization (Barad 2003). Modernist attempts to epistemologically separate subject and object, in this view, making just as little sense as any form of ontological anthropocentrism. Instead, feminist new materialism's focus on a nondualistic "epistem-ontology" (Barad 1996, p. 118) opens up ways to expanding the diversity of social bonding and community building and confronts us with new challenges for the regulation of social relations. This holds especially true, when relationships are not only transgressing traditional categorizations or species boundaries but connecting biological and technological actors, thus linking the carbon and silicon spheres. Analysing current trends in sex-robotics, I will highlight the paradox that, even though sex robots seemingly reinforce heteronormative gender dichotomies by imitating exaggerated pornographic stereotypes in appearance and behaviour, they also deconstruct traditional man/machine-dualisms—and doing so, open up paths for new constellations of trans-species partnerships beyond "carbon-chauvinism" (Sagan 1973) and the dictate of heteronormativity.

1. Ontologies of Love

Technology is always entangled in structures of power, and it is never gender neutral (e.g., (Barad 1996, 2003; Bath 2014a; Ernst and Horwath 2014; Haraway 1988, 2004; Oudshoorn and Pinch 2003; Rommes 2002, 2011; Wajcman 1991, 2004)). While this is obvious for products like deodorants, shavers, clothing, etc., that explicitly address customers of a certain gender, it also holds true for seemingly gender-neutral articles like computers, cars, or smart homes (Berg 1999; van Oost

2003). Far from being inherent to those 'things in themselves,' gender is constantly produced and reproduced through the principles guiding their design and subsequent social interactions during their use (Strathern 1988), thus binding together explicit and implicit notions of gendering in so-called "gender scripts" (Akrich 1992; Bath 2014a; van Oost 2003; Woolgar 1990). These scripts consist of built-in features assigning specific competences and delegating responsibilities to their intended users (Akrich 1992, p. 208); see also (Oudshoorn et al. 2005, p. 86; Rommes 2002, p. 18).

As for the sex robots that are currently developed, saying that they are gendered seems a truism. Mirroring a strong Eurocentric male gaze, their design takes semantic coding and stereotyping along hegemonic gender lines to the extreme, basically reducing 'robot companions' to large-breasted Barbie dolls with glimpses of artificial intelligence (e.g., (Truecompanion n.d.; RealbotiX n.d.a)). The 'inner values,' as praised on one producer's homepage, consist in little more than being always "ready to talk or play" (Truecompanion n.d.). This renaissance of male hegemonic ambition and the demand for female submissiveness (or, as some authors put it, "toxic masculinity" (Connell and Messerschmidt 2005; Gildea 2017)) appears as a severe setback for feminist efforts to achieve equality for all humans. Accordingly, the *Campaign Against Sex Robots* denounces the construction of "machines in the form of women or children for use as sex objects, substitutes for human partners or prostituted persons" (CASR n.d.) in the strongest terms.

These moral issues of course need to be addressed and, hopefully, they will eventually be resolved. However, I would like to put them aside for the time being and instead point out that the argument made by the *Campaign Against Sex Robots* takes one idea for granted: that sexual relationships between humans and robots are in fact possible. This statement needs some elaboration, since Kathleen Richardson and others have argued repeatedly, that there could be no such thing as sex between humans and robots. If sex is a co-experience, involving a mutual, parallel, and simultaneous experience between humans who are radically different from humanmade artefacts, then it follows that penile, digit, or oral penetration of an object does not constitute sex. This is the case whether the penetrated 'object' is in fact an objectified human being or an anthropomorphized object (Gildea and Richardson 2017).

At first glance, the argument sounds convincing. In fact, from a morally informed point of view, it is flawless. Yet it describes only a small sector of social reality. That becomes clear when, a bit later in the same article, Richardson and Gildea contrast this limited version of sex ("a co-experience ... between humans") to masturbation ("a sexual experience you have alone") and rape ("using a human being like they were a sexual instrument/sexual assault"), arguing that sex with robots cannot be "sex" because "dolls and robots do not have sexed bodies which include reproductive organs, hormones and are not part of a living species" (ibid.). The line of argument is basically ontological, defining 'real sex' along a fixed set of distinctive features. Accordingly, unreal sex, or rather 'not sex' is characterized by the lack of them.

[T]here is no subjectivity behind those glassy eyes. There is no mind with which the human partner can relate. There is a physical form, but no embodied consciousness. There may be a voice, but no internal dialogue. That voice may imply feelings, but they do not express a psychological reality. One can no more relate to a sex robot or sex doll than to a ventriloquist's dummy (except at least we know that behind the scenes the ventriloquist's dummy is being manipulated by human hand(s) without it being mystified as 'neutral' technology) (Gildea and Richardson 2017).

Now, what is the real point here? Obviously, Gildea and Richardson argue in favor of an absolute—one might even say transcendental—definition of sex. The argument is rooted in a decidedly Eurocentric, anthropocentric, and 'biocentric' position and takes things for granted that are anything but ontologically indisputable. While most readers probably agree that what Gildea and Richardson define as sex *is* a wonderful thing to happen, many of us are also aware that not all sexual experiences are equally enjoyable for everybody involved. Many of us probably remember sexual encounters, which, in retrospect, we might have preferred not to have had. Many of us experienced bad sex without considering it bordering on rape. Human sexuality was and is a broad field (Preciado 2000) and, unfortunately, the wonderful "mutual, parallel, simultaneous experience" was over large parts of human history and for the majority of humans probably the exception rather than the rule (Foucault 1993; Muchembled 2008).

What, then, would be a less normative, more manageable definition of sex? Or, rather, of love? Let me put the question differently: Does loving and feeling loved necessarily require its object to 'love back'? Or does it suffice, when the loving person *assumes* that their love is shared? I am leaning towards the latter. David Levy, one of the most outspoken advocates of robot sex, once predicted that within few decades, marriages between humans and robots would be widespread and perfectly normal (Levy 2007, p. 150). This bold statement obviously does not account for the fact that 'marriages' between humans are much more than just a vow of trying to make a relationship last. They bind together not just the bridal couple (or triple, or *n*-ple) but their respective families as well, thus creating complex networks of relatives and in-laws. However, we do not have to go that far to question the necessity of mutuality in loving relationships. Our love for pets and the manifold forms of objectophilia clearly show that the reality of our feelings does not rely on their reciprocation. I do like to believe that my dog in some way or the other loves me, but of course I will never find out, if that is true in an 'objective' sense. That, however, does not change the reality of *my* feelings nor does it deny the very existence of an affectionate relationship *between* us. I may well be just using the dog as a mirror projecting my own feelings and attitudes back on me. Yet, that does not affect the fact that these feelings result from an interaction with someone or something that is clearly not me. All moral considerations put aside, I therefore suggest a reformulation of the fundamental question. Instead of asking, if robots will ever love us back, we should rather analyze *how* sexual or emotional scripts may evoke human attachment to a robot. Obviously, people can develop durable relationships with all kinds of counterparts. I have argued elsewhere (Kubes 2019) that, whereas easily identifiable anthropomorphic features may facilitate the establishment of emotional bonds, almost any kind of "anthropomorphic anchoring point" (ibid.) will do. Therefore, while it may well be true that robots will never 'love' us—that does not mean that we cannot develop true feelings for them. In fact, a recent study at Stanford University suggests that participants of different genders were measurably aroused when touching a robot in the 'off-limits' parts of its body (as compared to only pointing at them or touching its hand or neck (Blakemore 2016)). This does not imply that the participants in the study had sexual thoughts about the robot or were sexually stimulated in any way, but there seemed to have been a strong tendency "to treat the robot like it had social rules that applied to it" (ibid.). These findings are consistent with assumptions from phenomenology. Merleau-Ponty (1964) pointed out that an "unseparated ontology" ("*ontologie non séparée*") does not necessarily imply two discrete sentient bodies but may rest on any form of interaction allowing for the reversibility of the sentient and the sensed ("*sensant et sensible*"; ibid. 188). This "indirect ontology" ("*ontologie indirecte*" (De Saint-Aubert 2006, p. 201)) creates meaning from the interplay of entities lacking solid ontological ground. It can also occur between a mind and its thoughts on a (solid or imagined) object. Spike Jonze's movie *Her* (2013), in which a man falls in love with the virtual assistant on his cell phone, played convincingly on the theme that the body is not important at all when it comes to humans falling in love.

Further narrowing down the question of the possibility of affective relationships between humans and (sex) robots, this means that both sides of the equation—humans *and* robots—are to be thought of as emergent subject/objects, which, in their actual form, only come into being as contingent actants in an ad hoc "assemblage" (Bennett 2005). Not being agents in and out of themselves, they rather represent what Diana Coole called "agentic capacities" (Coole 2005). They allow for the kind of performative metaphysics or "onto-epistem-ology" (Barad 2003, p. 829) that lay the symbolic-material ground for an "agential realism" (Barad 1996, 2003).

2. Feminist New Materialism, ANT, OOO, Diffraction and Robots

Western thought has settled in, well believing that humans are inherently different from everything around us. The assumption became even more powerful, when, from the 17th century onward, the religious framework that had governed science before, was bit by bit substituted for a secular one.

Scientists now no longer held that it was man's God-given mission to "fill the earth and subdue it," and to "rule over the fish in the sea and the birds in the sky and over every living creature that moves the ground" (Genesis 1:28), yet the Cartesian disjunction of *res cogitans* and *res extensa* (Reinhardt 2016) further entrenched the fundamental opposition between the realms of the human and the nonhuman, between subject and object (Descola 2011). One might even go one step further and claim with Bruno Latour that this separation (or rather its immediate corruption) marks the very birth of modern society.

Latour famously defined modernity as a twofold ensemble of practices: one trying to create ontologically detached zones by processes of "cleaning" (Latour 2002b, p. 19); the other fashioning hybrids (or networks) of nature and culture by a move Latour calls "translation" (Latour 2002a). Now the major problem, as Latour describes it, lies precisely in modernity's seeming success. The interaction of human subjects with the material world constantly generates chimeras that are neither subject nor object but something in-between—or rather both: holes in the ozone layer (Latour 2002b, p. 7), speed bumps (Latour 1994, p. 36), the Berlin key (Latour 1993), etc. Therefore, in order to really understand our being-in-the-world, we have to consider that the world *cannot* be neatly divided into (human) subjects and (material) objects, but contains an ever-growing portion of hybrids or "quasi-objects" (Serres 1987) that collapse the differentiation between the social and the material worlds, between nature and culture, between mind and matter. It is important to stress that these hybrids are not just humanized things or reified humans, but constitute an ontological order of their own. Consequently, instead of analyzing our intricately tangled world through the bifocal lens of modernity's subject–object dualism, Latour calls for a three-dimensional approach, complementing the two poles of the system by hitherto forbidden interbreeding of the 'soft' and the 'hard' components of nature and culture (2002b, p. 75).

This has severe implications for research, both in the natural sciences and the humanities. Knowledge—no matter on what—becomes inextricably *situated* by specific "agential cut[s|" (Barad 2007, p. 185). Agency in such "programs of action" (ibid.) is at least partly detached from humans and instead thought of as shared by an "association of actants" (Latour 1994, p. 35). 'Objects' are no longer passively waiting for an intentional 'subject' to manipulate them. Rather, they "mediate action" (Verbeek 2005, p. 131) and thus take any notion of an individuated subject acting on equally stable matter *ad absurdum*. In a similar—yet not quite the same—fashion, feminist new materialism proposes a nonessentializing approach to ontology and privileges (Deleuze and Guattari 1984, p. 4) the *production* (or *"enregistrement")* of the social over its *construction*.

This (re)turn to matter originates from a critical assessment of the linguistic turn and its insistence on the prevalence of discourse over existence. Karen Barad thoroughly explores the "representationalist" tradition (2003, p. 805), describing it as resting upon three problematic separations: subject/object, representation/thing, and epistemology/ontology. Taken for granted by representationalism, these separations imply the possibilities of a neutral observer position, of objective representations, and of an unobstructed access to knowledge. None of this, of course, should be taken as given. Things, as we all perfectly know, all too often seem to have a mind of their own. Jane Bennett (2010) hits a similar vein, when she argues that matter is imbued with a vitality or liveliness allowing it to shape the ways we interact with it. She calls this capacity "thing-power": Thing-power gestures toward the strange ability of ordinary, man-made items to exceed their status as objects and to manifest traces of independence or aliveness, constituting the outside of our own experience (Bennett 2010, p. xvi).

Notwithstanding the above, feminist new materialism does *not* propose a wholesale renunciation of constructionism. It rather uses it as one of its cornerstones and a counterbalance to its materialist side. That way, it both emphasizes its discontinuity with earlier materialist theories (like for example Marxist historical materialism) and underscores the "co-constitution of material and discursive productions of reality" (Sanzo 2018). In feminist new materialism, the social, the cultural, and the material are not being thought of in terms of superstructure and base but as caught in transformations and interactions that literally stop at nothing: self, matter, space, time, cause, etc.—everything is subject to constant modification, variation, and reconsideration.

There are different strands of new materialism(s) that all build on Latour's seminal work which are not always easy to distinguish. I do hold, however, that they represent three clearly discernible schools of thought. Actor network theory (ANT) rightly proceeds from the assumption that nature and culture cannot (as in modernism's unsuccessful attempt) be completely separated. That is why it puts such emphasis on studying hybrids (or quasi-objects) being made up of both nature *and* culture. Object-oriented ontology (OOO), on the other hand, insists that *not all* entities are hybrids, claiming instead that there are objects which completely lack the 'cultural' element (such as the hydrogen and oxygen molecules in H_2O) and others that are, on the contrary, purely cultural (like the idea of a Judeo-Christian 'Europe') (Harman 2018, p. 57). In rejecting the idea that *everything* is a hybrid, OOO contends that a universal amalgamation would effectively *preserve* the very constituents (nature and culture) that ANT tries to get rid of (Harman 2018, p. 58). Therefore, while contending that there are (*some*) hybrids, OOO warns against limiting research to network relations alone. Instead, it puts some sort of a double *withdrawal* (physical *and* logical) at the base of its ontology (Harman 2018, p. 187). This, however, conflates physical and phenomenological dimensions and ultimately leads to a deep "antipathy in relations in favor of the things themselves" (Sheldon 2015, p. 194).

Feminist new materialism here adopts a more radical stance. If anything, it is *relational*, claiming that subjects and objects, ideas and matter, representations and things are not inhabiting clearly separable ontological spheres. Where OOO disregards epistemology as a lower-level instrument that only deals with composites involving at least one human constituent, feminist new materialism stresses its indispensability for the very generation of reality.

Thus, similar as they may be in many respects, the three branches of new materialism differ decidedly with regard to the role they assign to the association of things and relations. ANT focuses on networks and relations, OOO on things, and, most comprehensively, feminist new materialism on intra-active processes, in which relations precede their relata, which, in turn, modify these relations (and so on *ad infinitum*) (Sheldon 2015, p. 202). Crucial for this process is "that intra-actions are live" (ibid.). They do not interweave pre-existing objects, nor do they withdraw objects from our access. Rather, they play on the mutual constitution of relations and relata and emphasize their simultaneous co-constitution in an eternal ouroboros. As Sheldon emphatically puts it: *"Nature cannot preexist its construction"* (2015, p. 197; emphasis in the original), and ontology, one may add, cannot precede epistemology. Both are effects of the same process that has been described as "diffractive" by various authors (Barad 2007; Bath 2014b; Haraway 1992, p. 300). Central to the metaphor is that, in optics, rays of light can 'bend' around the corners of an obstacle and through interferential (or diffractive) effects enter the region lying in the obstacle's shadow. Already back in 1992, Donna Haraway pointed out that interference patterns differ radically from reflections (or, to use a more common term: representations). Diffraction is a mapping of interference, not of replication, reflection, or reproduction. A diffraction pattern does not map where differences appear, but rather map where the *effects* of differences appear ((Haraway 1992, p. 300); emphasis added).

In other words, we cannot observe diffraction where it actually originates (at the obstacle) but only where its *effects* become visible (in the shadow space). Karen Barad, building on Haraway's use of the term, employs the metaphor for describing her own methodological approach of reading insights through one another in attending to and responding to the details and specificities of relations of difference and how they matter. (...) [D]iffraction can serve as a useful counterpoint to reflection: both are optical phenomena, but whereas the metaphor of reflection reflects the themes of mirroring and sameness, diffraction is marked by patterns of difference (Barad 2007, p. 71). In contrast to reflection, diffraction marks differences *from within* and sees them as part of entangled processes. Therefore, it can focus on differences and relationalities rather than on sameness and mimesis. It does not require preexisting, separate entities but produces "diffraction/difference pattern[s]" by the "material practice of engagement as part of the world in its differential becoming" (ibid., p. 89).

Coming back to the dangling possibility of sex robots and robot sex, one lesson from feminist new materialism therefore is that anthropocentrism and mimesis do *not* have to be the guiding principles in those robots' construction and design. It would thus be fatal to simply abandon all definitory power to the still predominantly male-dominated disciplinary culture of the engineering sciences. Instead, queer interventions on robot sex can (and should!) contribute to nonhierarchical creative and interpretive construction processes that traverse, overlap, and cut across sexual potentials without fitting into a normative unit. Traversing and perforating sexual stereotypes, they might—this at least is my hope—ultimately lead to 'better' sex robots that increase their users' physical and emotional pleasure but refuse fixed identity attributions.

3. From Pygmalion to Harmony to RealDollX

The idea of creating an artificial human-like counterpart has been a powerful topos in Western literature (or, as some would have it, a "collective human obsession" (Trout 2017)) for at least two thousand years. Most famously, in Ovid's *Metamorphoses*, the Cypriot sculptor Pygmalion falls in love with one of his statues. After Pygmalion presented his offerings to the gods during the festive days of Venus, the ivory statue comes alive and Pygmalion marries her. Together, they have a daughter, Paphos (Ovid 2003, pp. 10, 243–97).

What as a short plotline sounds like a tale about love, purity, human genius, and divine intervention, at a closer look turns into a narrative about a misogynic endeavor, setting the stage for technocrats' dreams about marrying robots as well as for the feminist critique of the very attempt to build them. Today, Pygmalion probably would identify as an 'incel,' or involuntary celibate. Disappointed, afraid or repulsed by real woman and their 'vicious nature' ("*vitiis, quae (...) menti femineae natura dedit*"), he creates an ivory simulacrum that is *better* than the real thing. Pygmalion gives his statue forms so perfect that no naturally born woman could possess ("*sculpsit (...) formamque dedit, qua femina nasci nulla potest*"). When he eventually falls in love with the sculpture, he must know that she is not human. Still, he chooses to believe that she reciprocates his feelings. He kisses the statue and is sure his kisses are returned ("*oscula dat reddique putat*"). Then, during a festival honoring Venus, Pygmalion presents his offerings to the goddess and makes it very clear that, in his view, the order of art and nature has been reversed by his craftmanship. He informs the goddess that he is determined to remain a celibate unless he is given a woman "like my ivory (virgin)" ("*similis mea (...) eburnae*"). Accordingly, he does not just ask the gods to give him a wife, he specifically adds that they should take the statue he has made as the model after which this wife should be fashioned.

There is a striking difference to other ancient myths on artists and their art. Other than the grapes painted by Zeuxis or Dibutades' shadow portrait of his daughter's lover, Pygmalion's statue does not *imitate* anything. It does not strive to be as accurate a copy of nature as possible. On the contrary, it *improves* nature, restoring it the purity and virtuousness that real humans (that is: women) lack in his opinion. Pygmalion's ivory sculpture is not an image (*Abbild*) but an archetype (*Urbild*), a copy that precedes its original and renders any distinction between reality and representation useless, or, as Baudrillard would have it, a third order "*simulacrum*" (Baudrillard 1982) that brings itself into existence. Just like today's sex robots, Galatea is not a simple mirror of a human, it is an interpretation of what a human *could* be that moves "beyond the ephemeral subject–object divide" (Lee 2017, p. 5).

Pygmalion's sexist escapism has inspired authors, painters, and sculptors for centuries. Victor Stoichita provides an extensive account of the multifold variations of the theme, from Ovid right up to Alfred Hitchcock's *Vertigo* (Stoichita 2008). The idea of the artist actually generating his future wife by the sole means of his art seems to be a widely shared fantasy. Today, however, we are only two steps away from this fantasy becoming real. Advances in robotics and artificial intelligence (AI) make it seem only a matter of time until we build machines that will easily pass the Turing test, that will interact with humans on eye-level and that will satisfy our physical and emotional needs through a wide range of behavioral responses. Already today, computers have replaced call center agents so successfully that we often unknowingly communicate with them on the phone without noticing. As algorithms advance, it will become virtually impossible to tell whether we talk to another human being or a voice from a machine. To tell the truth, we do not seem to care too much about that. Thus, as far as the human pole of this kind of man–machine interaction is concerned, the difference between humans and machines already has become effectively irrelevant in many contexts.

However, despite the widespread attention sex robots receive by the media, fully functional androids are still a long way off. While impressive progress was made in the field of combat robots, research on sex robotics is still in its infancy. What is currently ready to hit the market is little more than an animatronic robotic head with an interchangeable magnetic face and built in AI, mounted on a silicon doll that can be bent into the desired position but cannot move on its own. In order to avoid dents, owners are instructed to store the doll in a hanging position when not in use. This is also true for *Harmony* and her robotic sister *Solana*, the most advanced 'sex robots' to be found these days—and the two examples that hardly have been absent from *any* recent media coverage of the topic.

Their manufacturers, Matt McMullen and *Abbyss Creations*, are very straightforward as to the limits of their project. Thus, the recently relaunched website of *realbotix.com* describes the company's mission as follows:

We're working to create the next generation of the well-known anatomically correct RealDolls, which we intend to blend with Artificial Intelligence, Robotics, touch sensors, internal heaters, virtual and augmented reality interfaces. These new dolls will have an animated face synchronized with an application that users can talk to and interact with. The purpose behind the project is to create an illusion, or alternative to reality when it comes to a relationship with a doll. These RealDolls will have the ability to listen, remember, and talk naturally, like a living person. They will have hyper-realistic features, warmth, and sensors that react to touch. When interacting with these dolls, we want users to ask themselves, "What is she thinking?" (Available online: https://realbotix.com/FAQ).

Much could be said about this mission statement from a feminist point of view; however, I want to stress only a few aspects that are most relevant in our context. First, even though *Harmony* is 'the face' of the public discourse on robot sex, the term 'sex robot' is oddly missing in the company's communication. Instead, robotics is mentioned as just one of several features that shall blend to create a *doll*, "users can talk to and interact with." What *Harmony* (or "RealDollX") really is, thus, is not a sex robot in the strict sense of the term. It is a sex *doll* with an animated head and artificial intelligence. That is a significant difference. A doll is only an equal counterpart, if and as long as its user actively *attributes* that quality to it. There is nothing inherently *'almost human'* in it—and "doll" in fact sounds much less threatening than "robot." Accordingly, there is no such thing as a 'Campaign Against Sex Dolls'—and it is hard to imagine one going viral the way the *Campaign Against Sex Robots* did. Second, the purpose behind the project is explicitly described as creating an "illusion, or alternative reality"—not a *new* reality. Asked if they think "an AI RealDoll Robot will ever be able to love us back," the producers give a disarmingly honest answer: "We hope that we can at least simulate that. That's the goal. It is our thinking that if one feels loved, then one must be loved, deeply and genuinely" (Available online: https://realbotix.com/FAQ).

Love, as understood here, is not Gildea's and Richardson's "mutual, parallel and simultaneous experience" (Gildea and Richardson 2017), rather it is something happening exclusively in the eye of the beholder. Freed from ontological restraints, it becomes a matter of interpretation—or, one might say: of epistemology. Finally, there is this strange statement that the doll's features are "anatomically correct" but "hyper-realistic." Anatomically correct here probably means that orifices a (male) user might want to use for sexual purposes are where he would expect them to be and share certain features with the corresponding parts of the female body. More interesting, therefore, is the aspect of hyper-realism. Obviously, *Realbotix*' goal is not to simply depict or copy reality but to distort and to exaggerate it, and this does not have to stop at the human form and its limitations but can (and maybe should) go well beyond it.

Now, the dolls, on which *Harmony's* robotic head is to be mounted, may be impressive from an artistic perspective. From a feminist point of view, they are—there is no other way to say it—horrific. The same is true for the accompanying app that comes as a female avatar designed to serve as an interface to the robotic head. Both can be 'customized'—meaning that the client can choose from a selection of skin and lip types, labia, pubic hair (trimmed, 'natural,' shaved), nipple shades, breast sizes (all of them perfectly round and oddly defying gravity), and so on. Currently, the selection is pretty much limited to idealized forms doing little to hide their roots in pornographic fantasies. Hermaphrodite versions or 'Avatars' are possible; however, the company clearly has boundaries as to manufacturing, for example, sex animals (Lee 2017) or dolls representing children or celebrities. The accompanying app additionally allows one to create a "persona" that best suits the customer. Here, the user can choose from a list of personality traits that affect the way the doll behaves. The number of available personality traits, however, seems to have lost some of its variability over the course of the last two years. While the 2017 prototype of the app still had eighteen qualities to choose from ("intense, unpredictable, moody, shy, jealous, insecure, intellectual, helpful, quiet, talkative, kind, innocent, sexual, adventurous, affectionate, imaginative, sense of humor, happy" (Twitter 2017)), the 2019 version is down to only twelve ("affectionate, spiritual, unpredictable, jealous, intellectual, insecure, moody, sensual, cheerful, funny, helpful, talkative" (RealbotiX n.d.b)).

From a gender perspective, one would prefer to not even think about the heteronormative stereotyping clichés dominating the field (and its media coverage) in the first place, but again, Realbotix has produced (as they call it) "The World's Finest Love Dolls" (realbotix.com) since 1997. Thus, they are entering the field of sex robotics not as innocent newbies but as a company that has played the field of silicon sex dolls for decades. This is where their expertise lies and this is also what largely defines their target group. Therefore, I think it is a fatal mistake, when feminists discussing sex robots and robot sex take the appearance of Realbotix' dolls as a call to adopt a fundamentally negative attitude from the very start. It clearly resembles earlier feminist critiques of pornography focusing on the most shocking images available in an attempt to deny the very existence of a thing like feminist pornography (e.g., (Dworkin 1989; Morgan 1980; Schwarzer 1994)). Also, just as back then, the critique ultimately contributes to a further solidification of moral principles building on a dualistic order of the sexes. Even if the robots/dolls that are built today give only a very small group of male customers a chance to indulge in their sexual fantasies, that does not make the technology behind them a bad thing. True sexual liberation cannot stop at women (Rubin 1984). In the long run, it must also include men and everybody between and beyond. No matter if we focus on the dolls' exaggerated physical features or on the presumed long-term effects of sex robots on the fabric of gender relationships or on social power structures in general, confining ourselves to those aspects alone, we are negligently giving away the chance to play a part in shaping a technology with the potential of actually improving many people's lives.

Pleasure is not a bad thing. And I do not think that—generally speaking—there is anything wrong with reaching it by technological means. Just to give a well-documented example: the absolute number of female orgasms in the West obviously has multiplied over the last decades. This is not the least due to the increased acceptance and availability of sex toys. Recent research suggests that, for example, in the U.S. today, more than one in two women owns and uses a vibrator (Herbenick et al. 2009). When Kinsey published his report in 1953, their use was not "appreciable" and found (or admitted) by less than 1% of the informants. Some twenty years later, the Hite report showed this number to have increased to slightly above 14% (ibid.). From here to more than 50% in 2008 was a long way to go. Why did it take so long? One likely reason is that product development and design were almost exclusively left to male engineers and designers. And their ideas, to put it mildly, may not always have reflected women's ideas about what a sex toy should do and what it should look like.

Still in the 1990s, vibrators seemed to fall only in one of two groups: the horribly realistic replica of a penis (remaining a niche product for a sexually adventurous subculture), or disguised as a medical product and sold euphemistically as 'massage device.' It was only after *Sex and the City's* 'rabbit episode' in 1998, that—with a 'buzz,' so to speak—vibrators became mainstream. In a tribute to 20 years of the western world having become a "Vibrator Nation" (Comella 2017), even the conservative *Forbes* magazine claimed that the rabbit vibrator "ushered in a new era of sexual consumerism, one in which female shoppers boldly strutted into sex-toy stores looking to purchase the vibrator they'd seen on *Sex and the City*" *(Comella 2018)*.

There is no question that taking vibrators out of the shadows was an important step towards female empowerment and sexual satisfaction beyond heterosexual intercourse. The rabbit and its successors helped millions of women to a better sex life and the development did not stop at the unexpected success of a single product. Today, women can choose from a huge selection of vibrators in all shapes and colors in virtually any drugstore, where they are as openly on display as condoms or lubricants. There are also many other sex toys for women that simultaneously suck, push, rub, lick, vibrate and have nothing in common with the visual appearance and functionality of human genitalia, but nevertheless lead to new forms of female self-determined pleasure.

For men, on the other hand, there is nothing even remotely comparable. Of course, there *are* masturbation aids and sex dolls. However, it is hard to think of anybody wanting to be even loosely associated with them. Entering the search string "masturbator for men" on the webpage of a large online shop and scrolling through the results requires both a firm trust in the good in man *and* a strong stomach. The image that comes to mind when we think of a person actually buying and using a product like the "MissGem-Silicone-Lifelike-Realistic doll for men" is that of a person who has serious problems. Thus, there is a significant discursive imbalance regarding technological aids for sexual pleasure. Whereas vibrators are widely accepted as a symbol of female self-empowerment and a liberated sexuality, sex dolls, to put it bluntly, are considered a surrogate for pitiable "loser[s]" (Wennerscheid 2019, p. 123) who are afraid of real women. In movie analogies, it is *Lars and the Real Doll* (2007) instead of *Sex and the City*. The social framework the users of sex dolls inhabit is commonly considered as one of loneliness, isolation, and uninhibited consumerism.

I insist that it would not have to be like that. Sex robots leaving the beaten track of pornographic mimicry and sexist hyperfemininization might, in the end, equally contribute to liberated, transversal, self-empowered new forms of sexual pleasure beyond fixed heteronormative normalizations. After all, sex robots epitomize the decoupling of sexual craving from biological/social sex and/or gender and hold the potential for a radical pluralization of desire relations that no longer excludes nonmainstream forms of sexuality. To realize this potential, however, producers will eventually have to come up with some new design ideas. Vibrators, as we all have learned over the last twenty years, do not have to look like penises. Quite the contrary: they only became mainstream after their design had clearly moved away from naturalistic depictions of male genitalia. Transferring this knowledge to the field of robot sex, the obvious question we have to ask is: why should a sex robot look like a human?

Today, photographs from the RealDoll factory show long rows of female dolls hanging from rails on metal hooks. It looks like a scene from a pornographic slaughterhouse, an image, perfectly adding to the dystopian fears of the adversaries of robot sex. Yet again, modelling bodies after male pornographic fantasies is *not* the only (and certainly not the best) way to design a sex robot. It is my hope that eventually producers will thoroughly reconsider their design options. Starting from the scratch, they might define what the robot shall be able to *do* (instead of what it shall *be like*). If, at the end of this process, form really *follows* function, the result will not look anything near to today's sex robots. Not more, for sure, than today's vibrators resemble their lifelike ancestors from the 20th century. The underlying technology itself is neither good nor bad. It is up to us to appropriate it and to explore its utopian potential for different nonmainstream sexual encounters between—among others—consenting humans and machines.

4. Conclusions

The critique of sex robots and robot sex is characterized by rigorous uprightness, frequently combined with prudery, moral outrage, and sometimes all-too-hasty assumptions. Many of the arguments put forward against robot sex are logically unsound and can easily be interpreted contrary to the conclusions intended by their authors. If, for example, it is argued that treating robots as objects makes us more likely to objectify other humans, then one could just as convincingly reason that being able to show empathy with a machine should actually *increase* our empathy with our fellow human beings. In addition, if we claim that robot sex equals slavery or prostitution, we ultimately equip the robots with about just that minimal amount of 'human-ness' that robot sex' critics see as a prerequisite for a truly loving relationship. On the other hand, sex robots are neither a one-size-fits-all cure for loneliness, nor are they designated sex teachers that, as Levy once had it, "will turn receptive students into virtuoso lovers" and wipe bad sex from the face of the earth (Levy 2007, p. 307). It is interesting to see how critics and advocates of sex robots share the same false ontological assumptions in assigning almost transcendental qualities to relational agents. In fact, sex robots *may* accomplish all of the above—but only as one emerging and everchanging side of the equation.

Feminist new materialism has convincingly argued that what a thing ultimately 'is,' is how it *evolves* from concrete *intra-actions*. Accordingly, sex robots are neither *inherently* evil, nor do they necessarily add to the suppression of minorities or represent hegemonic masculinity at its worst.

Critics are absolutely right when they attack the way the female body is stereotypically exaggerated in the dolls and machines that currently dominate the field of sex robotics. Here, some sort of counterbalancing action is indeed required. However, instead of just denouncing those design aberrations as expressions of toxic masculinity and refusing any further debate, a much more effective way to fight them would be to become actively involved in future design decisions. The sex robot industry, to this day, is almost exclusively male-dominated and characterized by a male gaze. Even in pornography, the number of women in decision-making positions is higher than in sex robotics (Lee 2017). It should not come as a surprise, therefore, that its products do not mirror the huge variability of sexual practices and desires that govern our everyday lives.

The narrative of sex robots is just crossing from the realm of fiction into the material world. It is therefore all the more important for feminists and queer scholars not to refuse dialogue. It is about time to no longer leave the field to male engineers and their heteronormative fantasies but to become part of a concerted effort to explore "diffractive design" options (Bath 2014b) for sex robots from a gender-queer perspective. Instead of retreating into the growlery, lamenting the dystopian 'pygmalionization' of gender relations and sexual practices, we should strive for a sex-positive utopian future, playing an active role in the creation of post-gender pleasure robots and doing our part in changing the narratives about sex, love, and robots.

Funding: This research received no external funding.

Conflicts of Interest: The author declares no conflict of interest.

References

Akrich, Madeline. 1992. The De-Scription of Technical Objects. In *Shaping Technology/Building Society: Studies in Sociotechnical Change*. Edited by Wiebe E. Bijker and John Law. Cambridge: MIT Press, pp. 205–24.

Barad, Karen. 1996. Meeting the Universe Halfway: Realism and Social Constructivism without Contradiction. In *Feminism, Science, and the Philosophy of Science*. Edited by Lynn Hankinson Nelson and Jack Nelson. Dordrecht: Kluwer Press, pp. 161–94.

Barad, Karen. 2003. Posthumanist Performativity: Toward an Understanding of How Matter Comes to Matter. *Signs: Journal of Women in Culture & Society* 28: 801–31.

Barad, Karen. 2007. *Meeting the Universe Halfway: Quantum Physics and the Entanglement of Matter and Meaning*. Durham: Duke University Press.

Barraclough, Shanee. 2018. Ethico-onto-epistem-ological becoming. *Qualitative Research in Psychology* 15: 375–80. [CrossRef]

Bates, Laura. 2017. The Trouble with Sex Robots. *New York Times*. July 17. Available online: https://www.nytimes.com/2017/07/17/opinion/sex-robots-consent.html (accessed on 13 April 2019).

Bath, Corinna. 2014a. Searching for Methodology: Feminist Technology Design in Computer Science. In *Gender in Science and Technology. Interdisciplinary Approaches*. Edited by Waltraud Ernst and Ilona Horwath. Bielefeld: Transcript, pp. 57–78.

Bath, Corinna. 2014b. Diffractive Design. In *GENDER-UseIT. HCI, Usability und UX unter Gendergesichtspunkten*. Edited by Nicola Marsden and Ute Kempf. Berlin: De Gruyter, pp. 27–36.

Baudrillard, Jean. 1982. *Der Symbolische Tausch und der Tod*. München: Matthes & Seitz.

Bennett, Jane. 2005. The Agency of Assemblages and the North American Blackout. *Public Culture* 17: 445–65. [CrossRef]

Bennett, Jane. 2010. *Vibrant Matter: A Political Ecology of Things*. Durham and London: Duke University Press.

Berg, A. J. 1999. A Gendered Socio-Technical Construction: The Smart House. In *The Social Shaping of Technology*. Edited by Judy Wajman and Donald MacKenzie. Buckingham: Open University Press, pp. 301–13.

Beschorner, Thomas. 2017. Dingsbums—Sex mit der Maschine. *Die Zeit*. June 6. Available online: https://www.zeit.de/wirtschaft/2017--06/sex-roboter-gummipuppe-messe (accessed on 13 April 2019).

Blakemore, Erin. 2016. Touching Robots Can Turn Humans on, Study Finds. *The Washington Post*, April 4.

Bosteels, Bruno. 1998. From Text to Territory: Félix Guattari's Cartographies of the Unconscious. In *Deleuze and Guattari: New Mappings in Politics, Philosophy, and Culture*. Edited by Eleanor Kaufman and Kevin Jon Heller. Minneapolis: University of Minnesota Press, pp. 145–74.

Butler, Judith. 1990. *Gender Trouble: Feminism and the Subversion of Identity*. New York and London: Routledge.

CASR. n.d. Campaing Against Sex Robots. Available online: https://campaignagainstsexrobots.org/about/ (accessed on 23 March 2019).

Comella, Lynn. 2017. *Vibrator Nation: How Feminist Sex-Toy Stores changed the Business of Pleasure*. Durham and London: Duke University Press.

Comella, Lynn. 2018. 20 Years Later: How The 'Sex and The City' Vibrator Episode Created A Lasting Buzz. *Forbes*. August 7. Available online: https://www.forbes.com/sites/lynncomella/2018/08/07/20-years-later-how-the-sex-and-the-city-vibrator-episode-created-a-lasting-buzz/ (accessed on 26 March 2019).

Connell, Raewyn W., and James W. Messerschmidt. 2005. Hegemonic Masculinity. Rethinking the Concept. *Gender and Society* 19: 829–59. [CrossRef]

Coole, Diana. 2005. Rethinking Agency: A Phenomenological Approach to Embodiment and Agentic Capacities. *Political Studies* 53: 124–42. [CrossRef]

De Saint-Aubert, Emmanuel. 2006. *Vers une Ontologie Indirecte: Sources et Enjeux Critiques de L'appel à L'ontologie chez Merleau-Ponty*. Paris: J. Vrin.

Deleuze, Gilles, and Félix Guattari. 1984. *Anti-Oedipus: Capitalism and Schizophrenia*. London: Athlone.

Descola, Philippe. 2011. *Jenseits von Natur und Kultur*. Berlin: Suhrkamp.

Dworkin, Andrea. 1989. Pornography is a Civil Rights Issue: 1986. In *Letters from a War Zone: Writings 1976–1989*. New York: E.P. Dutton, pp. 276–307.

Eco, Umberto. 1987. *Lector in Fabula: Die Mitarbeit der Interpretation in Erzählenden Texten*. München: Hanser.

Ernst, Waltraud, and Ilona Horwath, eds. 2014. *Gender in Science and Technology: Interdisciplinary Approaches*. Bielefeld: Transcript.

FAZ. 2018. Sexroboter zum Ausprobieren: Houston verbietet Eröffnung von "Roboter-Bordell". *Frankfurter Allgemeine Zeitung*. October 4. Available online: https://www.faz.net/aktuell/gesellschaft/menschen/houston-verbietet-eroeffnung-von-roboter-bordell-15820308.html (accessed on 13 April 2019).

Foucault, Michel. 1993. *Der Wille zum Wissen*. Frankfurt am Main: Suhrkamp.

Gee, Tabi Jackson. 2017. Why Female Sex Robots Are More Dangerous Than You Think. *The Telegraph*, July 5.

Gildea, Florence. 2017. The Logic of Toxic Masculinity: Pornography and Sex Dolls. Available online: https://campaignagainstsexrobots.org/2017/05/23/the-logic-of-toxic-mascunlinity-pornography-and-sex-dolls-by-florence-gildea/ (accessed on 25 July 2019).

Gildea, Florence, and Kathleen Richardson. 2017. Sex Robots—Why We Should Be Concerned. Available online: https://campaignagainstsexrobots.org/2017/05/12/sex-robots-why-we-should-be-concerned-by-florence-gildea-and-kathleen-richardson/ (accessed on 25 July 2019).

Guarino, Ben. 2018. New report finds no evidence that having sex with robots is healthy. *The Washington Post*. June 4. Available online: https://www.washingtonpost.com/news/speaking-of-science/wp/2018/06/04/theres-no-evidence-that-having-sex-with-robots-is-healthy-new-report-finds/?noredirect=on&utm_term=.05cab48d7921 (accessed on 13 April 2019).

Haraway, Donna. 1988. Situated Knowledges: The Science Question in Feminism and the Privilege of Partial Perspective. *Feminist Studies* 14: 575–99. [CrossRef]

Haraway, Donna. 1992. The Promises of Monsters: A Regenerative Politics for Inappropriate/d Others. In *Cultural Studies*. Edited by Lawrence Grossberg, Cory Nelson and Paula A. Treichler. New York: Routledge, pp. 295–33.

Haraway, Donna. 2004. Morphing in the Order. Flexible Strategies, Feminist Science Studies, and Primate Revision. In *The Donna Haraway Reader*. New York and London: Routledge, pp. 199–222.

Harman, Graham. 2018. *Object-Oriented Ontology: A New Theory of Everything*. London: Pelican Books.

Herbenick, Debra, Michael Reece, Stephanie Sanders, Brian Dodge, Annahita Ghassemi, and J. Dennis Fortenberry. 2009. Prevalence and Characteristics of Vibrator Use by Women in the United States: Results from a Nationally Representative Study. *The Journal of Sexual Medicine* 2009: 1857–66. [CrossRef] [PubMed]

Kerner, Ian. 2018. What the Sex Robots Will Teach Us. *CNN*. March 12. Available online: https://edition.cnn.com/2016/12/01/health/robot-sex-future-technosexuality/index.html (accessed on 13 April 2019).

Kubes, Tanja. 2019. Bypassing the Uncanny Valley: Postgender Sex Robots and Robot Sex beyond Mimicry. In *Anthology Feminist Philosophy of Technology. Techno: Phil—Aktuelle Herausforderungen der Technikphilosophie*. Edited by Janina Loh and Marc Coeckelbergh. Stuttgart: J.B. Metzler Verlag.

Latour, Bruno. 1993. *La Clef de Berlin et Autres Leçons d'un Amateur de Sciences*. Paris: La Decouvert.

Latour, Bruno. 1994. On Technical Mediation: Philosophy, Sociology, Genealogy. In *Common Knowledge*. Durham: Duke University Press, vol. 3, pp. 29–37.

Latour, Bruno. 2002a. *Die Hoffnung der Pandora*. Frankfurt am Main: Suhrkamp.

Latour, Bruno. 2002b. *Wir Sind nie Modern Gewesen: Versuch einer Symmetrischen Anthropologie*. Frankfurt and Main: Fischer.

Lee, Jason. 2017. *Sex Robots: The Future of Desire*. Cham: Palgrave Macmillan.

Levy, David. 2007. *Love and Sex with Robots: The Evolution of Human-Robot Relationships*. New York: Harper Collins.

Merleau-Ponty, Maurice. 1964. *Le Visible et L'Invisible*. Paris: Gallimard.

Miethge, Christiane. 2017. Homo Digitalis: Der digitale Höhepunkt. *Arte TV*. October 17. Available online: https://www.arte.tv/de/videos/072427-003-A/homo-digitalis/ (accessed on 25 July 2019).

Morgan, Robin. 1980. Theory and Practice: Pornography and Rape. In *Take Back the Night: Women on Pornography*. Edited by Laura Lederer. New York: William Morrow & Co, pp. 134–40.

Muchembled, Robert. 2008. *Orgasm and the West: A History of Pleasure from the Sixteenth Century to the Present*. Cambridge: Polity Press.

Oudshoorn, Nelly, and Trevor Pinch, eds. 2003. *How Users Matter. The Co-Construction of Users and Technologies*. Cambridge: MIT Press.

Oudshoorn, Nelly, Margo Brounds, and Ellen van Oost. 2005. Diversity and Distributed Agency in the Design and Use of Medical Video-Communication Technologies. In *Inside the Politics of Technology. Agency and Normativity in the Co-Production of Technology and Society*. Edited by Hans Harbers. Amsterdam: Amsterdam University Press, pp. 85–105.

Ovid. 2003. *Metamorphosen*. Studienausgabe Lateinisch Deutsch. Düsseldorf and Zürich: Artemis & Winkler.

Preciado, Beatriz. 2000. *Manifeste Contra-Sexuel*. Paris: Éditions Jacob-Duvernet.

RealbotiX. n.d.a. Available online: https://www.realdollx.ai (accessed on 29 April 2019).

RealbotiX. n.d.b. Available online: https://realbotix.com/ (accessed on 23 March 2019).

Reinhardt, Thomas. 2016. Der Körper als Palimpsest: Erinnerungstopographien zwischen Schrift und Leiblichkeit. In *Dem Körper eingeschrieben: Verkörperungen zwischen Leiberleben und kulturellem Sinn*. Edited by Matthias Jung, Michaela Bauks and Andreas Ackermann. Wiesbaden: Springer, pp. 109–21.

Richardson, Kathleen. 2015. The Asymmetrical 'Relationship': Parallels between Prostitution and the Development of Sex Robots. *SIGCAS Computers & Society* 45: 290–93. Available online: https://campaignagainstsexrobots.org/the-asymmetrical-relationship-parallels-between-prostitution-and-the-development-of-sex-robots/ (accessed on 25 July 2019).

Richardson, Kathleen. 2016. Sex Robot Matters. *IEEE Technology and Society Magazine*, June. 46–53.

Rogowska-Stangret, Monika. 2017. Corpor(e)al Cartographies of New Materialism: Meeting the *Elsewhere* Halfway. *Minnesota Review* 88: 59–68. [CrossRef]

Rommes, Els. 2002. *Gender Scripts and the Internet: The Design and Use of Amsterdam's Digital City*. Enschede: Twente University Press.

Rommes, Els. 2011. Inclusion by Design. In *Technologies of Inclusion*. Edited by Knut Holtan Sorensen, Wendy Faulkner and Els Rommes. Trondheim: Tapir, pp. 129–46.

Rubin, Gayle. 1984. Thinking Sex: Notes for a Radical Theory of the Politics of Sexuality. In *Pleasure and Danger: Exploring Female Sexuality*. Edited by Carole Vance. Boston: Routledge & Kegan Paul, pp. 267–319.

Sagan, Carl. 1973. *The Cosmic Connection: An Extraterrestrial Perspective*. New York: Anchor Books, Doubleday.

Sanzo, Kameron. 2018. New Materialism(s). Available online: http://criticalposthumanism.net/new-materialisms/ (accessed on 23 March 2019).

Schmieder, Jürgen. 2019. Selbsttest: So ist es, ein Date mit einem Sex-Roboter zu haben. *Focus Online*. March 22. Available online: https://www.focus.de/digital/produkte/selbsttest-so-ist-es-eine-date-mit-einem-sex-roboter-zu-haben_id_10493878.html (accessed on 13 April 2019).

Schwarzer, Emma, ed. 1994. *PorNO: Opfer & Täter, Gegenwehr & Backlash, Verantwortung & Gesetz*. Köln: Kiepenheuer & Witsch.

Serres, Michel. 1987. *Der Parasit*. Frankfurt and Main: Suhrkamp.

Shaw, Adam. 2018. House votes to ban shipments of child sex robots. *Foxnews*. May 14. Available online: https://www.foxnews.com/politics/house-votes-to-ban-shipments-of-child-sex-robots (accessed on 13 April 2019).

Sheldon, Rebekah. 2015. Form/Matter/Chora: Object-Oriented Ontology and Feminist New Materialism. In *The Nonhuman Turn*. Edited by Richard Grusin. Minneapolis: University of Minnesota Press, pp. 193–222.

Sparrow, Robert. 2019. Would it be wrong to "rape" a sex robot? *ABC News*. March 15. Available online: https://www.abc.net.au/religion/would-it-be-wrong-to-rape-a-sex-robot/10848376 (accessed on 13 April 2019).

Stoichita, Victor I. 2008. *The Pygmalion Effect: From Ovid to Hitchcock*. London and Chicago: University of Chicago Press.

Strathern, Marilyn. 1988. *The Gender of the Gift: Problems with Women and Problems with Society in Melanesia*. Los Angeles and London: Berkeley.

Trout, Christopher. 2017. RealDoll's First Sex Robot Took Me to the Uncanny Valley. Available online: https://www.engadget.com/2017/04/11/realdolls-first-sex-robot-took-me-to-the-uncanny-valley/ (accessed on 13 April 2019).

Truecompanion. n.d. Available online: http://www.truecompanion.com/shop/faq (accessed on 23 March 2019).

Twitter. 2017. Available online: https://twitter.com/Guile_Lindroth/status/855235850820603904 (accessed on 29 April 2019).

van Oost, E. 2003. Materialized Gender. How Shavers Configure the Users' Femininity and Masculinity. In *How Users Matter. The Co-Construction of Users and Technologies*. Edited by Nelly Oudshoorn and Trevor Pinch. Cambridge: MIT Press, pp. 193–208.

Varley, Ciaran. 2018. Are sex robots just turning women into literal objects? *BBC*. April 6. Available online: https://www.bbc.co.uk/bbcthree/article/8bbe0749--62ee-40f9-a8ac-a2d751c174f6 (accessed on 13 April 2019).

Verbeek, Peter-Paul. 2005. Artifacts and Attachment: A Post-Script Philosophy of Mediation. In *Inside the Politics of Technology: Agency and Normativity in the Co-Production of Technology and Society*. Edited by Hans Harbers. Amsterdam: Amsterdam University Press, pp. 125–46.

Wajcman, Judy. 1991. *Feminism Confronts Technology*. Cambridge: Polity Press.

Wajcman, Judy. 2004. *TechnoFeminism*. Cambridge: Polity Press.

Weber, Christian. 2018. AI Love You: Sexroboter und Menschen: Kann das eine Liebesgeschichte werden? *Süddeutsche Zeitung*. September 29. Available online: https://projekte.sueddeutsche.de/artikel/wissen/sexroboter-kann-das-liebe-sein-e763870/?reduced=true (accessed on 13 April 2019).

Wennerscheid, Sophie. 2019. *Sex Machina: Zur Zukunft des Begehrens*. Berlin: Matthes & Seitz.

Woolgar, Steve. 1990. Configuring the User. The Case of Usability Traits. *The Sociological Review* 38: 58–99. [CrossRef]

© 2019 by the author. Licensee MDPI, Basel, Switzerland. This article is an open access article distributed under the terms and conditions of the Creative Commons Attribution (CC BY) license (http://creativecommons.org/licenses/by/4.0/).

MDPI
St. Alban-Anlage 66
4052 Basel
Switzerland
Tel. +41 61 683 77 34
Fax +41 61 302 89 18
www.mdpi.com

Social Sciences Editorial Office
E-mail: socsci@mdpi.com
www.mdpi.com/journal/socsci

www.ingramcontent.com/pod-product-compliance
Lightning Source LLC
LaVergne TN
LVHW071443100526
838202LV00088B/6791